The Art of Teaching Sunday School:

Preschool → Adult

LAURA R. LANGHOFF ARNDT

DEDICATION

To all the teachers of the Word as they do their most important job.

To God be the glory, great things He has done

CONTENTS

FOREWORD

Most churches today have some sort of educational programming that takes place on a Sunday morning. Research is clear however, that merely having a Sunday morning education time doesn't necessarily enhance faith maturation or correlate with characteristics of a healthy congregation – but Sunday schools that make use of effective educational methods does show these benefits. As Thom Rainer said – "Sunday School works. But only if we work Sunday School." (Rainer, High Expectations, pg. 47)

Laura Langhoff Arndt clearly understands this call to effective practices, and rightly recognizes that the teacher is a key ingredient in the delivery of an effective educational experience. Arndt does something unique in her approach, she takes what we know about brain development and develops a type of scope and sequence for a comprehensive parish educational process. From Narrative to Wisdom, Arndt weaves the practitioner through implementation strategies that, if carefully implemented, will align with the capacity and interests of the learners based upon their development stages.

There are better and worse ways to teach. The difference between talking and teaching is that teaching happens only if someone has learned, and there are things that a teacher can do that increases the potential for learning to happen. While this seems an obvious insight, churches seldom provide their volunteer teachers with resources to assist in their important role, leaving them to learn by trial and error and, in the process, to risk putting talking in the place of teaching. With this book, Arndt provides a resource that volunteer teachers can understand, while still providing insights into key factors which will contribute to creating learning in the lives of the participants.

This book, if used properly, will benefit the Sunday School teacher as well as the leadership of the congregation's educational efforts. The chapter on children's messages provides a valuable tool for pastors who too often deliver preludes to their sermons that are designed in ways that, while understandable to adults, has little content that children can understand. The sample lesson plans and tips for effective practices provide practical advice that aligns with the developmental characteristics for learners.

The Art of Teaching Sunday School helps leaders and teachers in our churches to strengthen one of our most important tools in carrying out the work of the church – our educational ministries.

Mark Blanke, EdD
Professor of Education, DCE Program Director
Concordia University, Nebraska

Foreword

PREFACE

This book shares the secrets of elementary education and child development with Sunday school teachers. Why? Because our Sunday schools enlist volunteer teachers with little or no training (Lohmeyer, 2015), and there is little provided to help train them. Maya Angelou said, "Do the best you can until you know better. Then when you know better, do better." With the amount of research done in education and the workings of the brain, we know better. It is time to support our volunteers in congregational or parish education and equip them for what we are asking them to do. By having a little more information, our Sunday school teachers and Bible study leaders, with the help of the Holy Spirit, can more confidently share the inspiring and loving stories of the Old Testament, the Life of Jesus, and the letters of the apostles to their congregations in ways that help them become more meaningful and memorable.

This is not the next great Sunday school curriculum and it doesn't talk about all the different aspects of program models or possible Christian crafts. This book is intended to provide insight for teaching volunteers how to help children and adults interact with information in a more meaningful way at their developmental level. It draws on my background as a professional educator with an M.A. in classroom instruction, years of experience in education, and a Director of Christian Education certification (Lutheran Church – Missouri Synod), to help pastors train their volunteers, and to provide support and encouragement to every one of them as they share the Bible with millions of young children, teenagers, and adults.

I give thanks to God for the gifts that He has showered upon me and for the courage to share them with a world that is becoming more hostile toward Christianity. I also thank Him for my family; my husband, Pastor Kevin Arndt, and his eight children and three grandchildren. Each one is special and unique and is forever in my heart.

INTRODUCTION

One of the Hebrew (causative) words for 'to teach' in the Bible is LAMAD and it means to *cause to learn*. Whether child or adult, that's what our goal is when leading or facilitating a Bible study. We want to cause people to learn something new or challenge them in some way so that, with the help of the Holy Spirit, their faith grows or deepens. There are four areas people (children and adults) change or grow through education (Kamp, 2011):

- **Skills** (they learn how to do something new)
- **Behavior** (they choose to do something differently)
- **Knowledge** (they have more information to apply to their lives)
- **Attitude** (they come away a changed person).

Education is a vital part of God's church as we are told in the Great Commission to baptize and teach (Matthew 28:16-20). Parents are to teach their children as they sit in their homes, or as they go by their way, when they lie down and when they rise up (Deuteronomy 6:7). Before there were books or Sunday school lessons, every parent was to tell the story of their people, our people. It's the story of a God who never turns away. As Russ Ramsey describes it in *Behold the Lamb of God* (2011),

> "It is a story of evil against good, of darkness locked in an epic struggle to snuff out the light forever. It is a tale filled with people in trouble, all living somewhere between wandering and homecoming, between devastation and restoration, between transgression and grace. Every mortal character in the story needs rescue, but they have all turned aside, and together they have become corrupt. After clearing away all the levels of intrigue, conflict, and suspense facing mankind, this story is a story of divine love. It is a story of the one true God calling a people his beloved, though they've lived in perpetual rebellion against him. Though their lives were a ruin of their own making, God swore a covenant oath to redeem them. Everything wrong with the world He would put right. He would remove their hearts of stone and give them hearts of flesh, putting a new spirit within them. And He would never, ever stop loving them."

This is the amazing story we are to pass down to our children so they can pass it down to their children.

To help parents pass down this story of salvation, congregations developed Sunday school programs, youth groups, opportunities for adult Bible study, etc. How can people share this story or parents pass the story down to their children if they do not know or understand it? They are their child's greatest influence and the cornerstone of a faithful home.

In a recent education insert for the LCMS *Reporter*, a study by the Institute for Religious Education at Concordia University, Nebraska stated that pastors report spending 23% of their time working on the educational ministries of the congregation. The same insert also challenged congregations to focus on lifelong learning and gave a list of the types of practices that "healthy" congregations exhibit (June, 2015). While these are all good things, the question is, if pastors are not trained educators and are not trained regarding education in the seminary, how are they to train the parents? How are they to train their volunteer teachers?

This book has been written for two simple reasons, the first being that most Sunday school teachers receive little or no training. It is not that they are not provided a curriculum. It is not that they are unfamiliar with Bible stories. It is that nobody knows how to effectively equip them. Pastors and other church professionals can be very helpful in providing background information about the Bible, history, or topics to be covered, but how does the volunteer translate that information to the appropriate age level? Sometimes teachers are given opportunities to go through the curriculum and ask questions, but for the most part, volunteers don't know what they don't know about educating the age group they teach, so they don't know what questions to ask.

The second reason, and the more serious of the two, is that one purpose in having a building that we call a church is to have a common place to encourage and equip Christians through sacramental worship and Bible study, so that we may then equip and bless our families with knowledge of the Bible and the confidence to go out into the world, live our faith, and share the Gospel of Jesus Christ. In order for this to happen, we must train those who teach and lead Bible study at any age.

Over the years, Sunday school has been simple education. Teachers follow the curriculum they are given, assuming that it will be adequate. The questions today are:

- Is what has been done for so long still working for children?
- Are our current methods of teaching adolescents and adults effective?
- How can we more appropriately prepare those who teach them, including our leaders?
- What is a good teacher of the faith?

The first chapter of this book is about how the brain develops or matures and learns. Without understanding how we learn as we mature, we miss out on opportunities to share in ways that people learn best. After the first chapter the book is broken into five stages of learning or spiritual development: Narrative, Knowledge, Understanding, Reason, and Wisdom.

In the Lutheran Church we call spiritual development *teaching the faith*. We teach people of all ages what the Bible says, and why we believe what we believe. Teaching the faith can begin at any age and can have a profound effect on faith in any number of ways. As teachers of the faith we may have students in a class who have had years of exposure to the Bible and those who have never owned or opened one at any age or in any class.

There is a distinction between spiritual development and faith. As we grow our ability to understand complex issues and themes grows; we find we can understand some of the deeper meanings in the Bible and the complexities of theology (the study of and attempt to understand God). We are able to question and discuss complex and often seemingly contrasting Biblical and theological issues. Our ability to understand, however, is not connected to our faith. Faith is a gift from the Holy Spirit that even newborn babies can have. Ironically, we can have our greatest faith when we are young.

To help describe the stages of faith development I've separated them into five categories: Narrative, Knowledge, Understanding, Reason, and Wisdom.

Narrative is the stage for children from preschool through second grade. These are the wonderful years when great stories turn into great learning; when they become a part of the child's world view. Young children become familiar with the Word of God by learning His stories and there are a lot of them! It's not important that they understand everything about them, it's not important that they can think deeply about them, but it's important that we lay the groundwork and they become familiar with them. It's not only God's story, it's their story.

Knowledge is the stage for children from third through fifth grade. It is the time of learning more detailed Biblical facts of the stories and talking about them, laying the groundwork for advanced study. Children at this age are seeing a bigger, more complex world and have questions. Who are the disciples and what was their purpose? What were the people in the Bible like? Who is Noah and what can we learn from his story? Where did Paul go on his journeys and what happened to him? They start asking who God is, why Jesus died for us, and who or what the Holy Spirit is. Going over the same stories they learned about when in the narrative stage, students see them as bigger and more complex than they were before and begin to understand more of the details.

Understanding is the stage of sixth through eighth grade; the confirmation years. It's at this stage that they begin to think more analytically. While still important to know, the facts become less important than why things happened. Students think more logically and notice when things don't make sense to them. Why did God flood the earth? Why were the people so evil? What does it mean to be righteous? Why does God need us to be holy? Couldn't God simply make everything okay? The implications of the stories begin to have much deeper meaning and we want to encourage questions. Students seek to understand the Bible more fully as it taps into how they feel or think about what they know about Scripture and what they are learning about the world.

Reason is the stage for ninth through twelfth grades and college students. It builds on the first three stages, using knowledge and understanding to dig deep and tries to see how what they know applies directly to their lives. In high school students begin searching for the truth of life, which is directly related to Scripture. A lot is going on in their bodies and lives at this time as they begin to become independent. They no longer want to be told what to do, think, or believe. They want to believe it on their own. They are developing their reason and judgment and deciding what is true or false. The world (and a lot of untruth) is at their feet, or more accurately, their fingertips. At this stage allowing them to ask, and answering their questions becomes very important. How do we do that? How do we ask questions that will get them to think? How do we challenge their faith so that they become comfortable and confident in it?

Wisdom is the stage of adulthood. The brain has fully matured, we know the stories, have thought about them and learned from them and have finally reached the point of wisdom. We're done! Not at all. The truly wise know that where faith is concerned, learning only ends once we are in the presence of the Lord. Only then will we truly understand. Teaching or learning as an adult, however, is different from when we were children or teenagers. It is in this stage that we shift from having to attend Bible study because we are told to by our parents, to wanting to learn. As He draws us to Him, we have a desire to know more and the only way we can do that is to dig deeper into Scripture.

How do adults learn? What keeps them coming back? Can how we teach affect their desire to learn more? How does one create an atmosphere that piques their interest, challenges their comfort in what they believe, and encourages them to continue coming back to learn more? The stories we've heard our whole lives, as an adult, become infinitely more fascinating and interesting. How do we equip and encourage people to teach as if they believe that? These questions are what this book is all about.

So, dear teacher of the faith, whether you teach five-year-olds, teenagers, or adults, this book is what you've been hoping for. It will give you confidence that whatever curriculum you have, you can use it to its fullest. It is time to set aside the dry read-a-story-and-paste-paper-together lessons for children or weak-question-obvious-answer studies for adults and begin something that will be meaningful to each child at every grade level, from preschool through adult.

Read on!

I praise you because I am fearfully and wonderfully made;
your works are wonderful,
I know that full well.

Psalm 139:14

Brain

CHAPTER 1

The Brain and Learning

To see intelligent design, we need to look no further than our own bodies, especially our brains! The brain is our most complicated organ. It is truly amazing! In *The Teenage Brain* (2015), Frances Jensen explains that "The brain changes as it grows, going through special stages that take advantage of the childhood years and the protection of the family, then, toward the end of the teen years, the surge toward independence. Human children and teens can imprint on experiences they have, and these can influence what they choose to do as adults."

There are two periods in life when the brain goes through a lot of change, the first few years of life and adolescence. As you can see from the picture, the brain develops from back to front. It isn't fully developed until

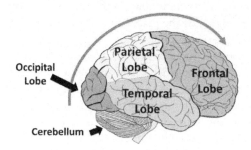

our middle 20s. The area that develops first is the primal brain, the cerebellum (motor patterning and coordination) and occipital lobe (visual cortex). Following is the parietal lobe (thought, memory, and learning) and temporal lobe (emotion and sexuality). Language is also located in the temporal lobe (Jensen, 2015). The last part of the brain to develop or mature is the frontal lobe. That's the part that houses risk assessment, judgment, insight, and impulse control.

While current brain research is not primarily for the purpose of education, brain-based education takes into account how the brain learns naturally and how its structure and function change at different stages of life (Froschl & Sprung, 2005). Contrary to what is often assumed, we don't think from a left (logic) or right (creative) brain nor do our brains function like a computer where certain areas hold certain processes or information. Thanks to the functional magnetic resonance imaging (fMRI) system, we can now see how blood flows in the brain when people do different cognitive tasks (National Research Counsil, 1999). It functions more as a whole with the hemispheres communicating with each other.

Recently, scientists have been looking into how our brains gather, process, and retain information (Caine & Caine, 1991). In his book, *Teaching with the Brain in Mind*, Eric Jensen (2005) states that "challenge, feedback, novelty (or originality), coherence (or consistency), and time are crucial ingredients for rewiring the brain." What does that mean? It means we learn best under certain conditions.

In *The Teenage Brain* (2015), Frances Jensen reveals that young brains are shaped by experience. Memories, with regard to how the brain learns, are not only parts of our life that we recall. They are everything our brains have experienced and learned throughout our lives. Jensen (2015) also shares the learning process, which is much the same for young and old brains. The brain receives information from the five senses (taste, touch, see, hear, smell) which is temporarily stored in short-term memory. Short-term memory is extremely active as it receives continuous input while we are awake. The information received is compared with existing memories to see if it is redundant or new. Redundant information is discarded and new information is sent to one of the places that stores long-term memories.

Jensen continues explaining that the transmission of sensory information is very quick, but not perfect. It can be interrupted and damage can occur. When this happens we fill in or connect what is lost with what we think makes sense, causing our memories to be incorrect. Learning occurs when different or exciting information is received and our brains are stimulated. Because the part of the brain that holds back excitement is developed last, young brains have more excitatory synapses than inhibitory synapses causing them to be ripe for learning. The more information is repeated, the stronger the neurons become and the connection becomes a well-worn path. The phrase "use it or lose it" is real. The more we recall information or use it again, the more deep-rooted or established it becomes.

It was once thought that we were born with a certain number of brain cells and lost them as we aged. We were stuck with the brains we got at birth and everything was downhill from there. Now we know that the brain is adaptable and we all have the opportunity to change and grow cognitively within our genetic make-up (Jensen, 2015). Jensen confirms that, based on how we respond to our environment, our brains are continually making new connections. While there may be certain stages of life when our brains learn best, learning does not end at any age. With special regard to Bible study, learning is not only for the young.

Brain and Memory

In his book *Brain Rules*, John Medina (2008), a developmental molecular biologist, shares what he defines as the 12 basic ways brains function, many of which will boost the religious education experience. While all of the rules are relevant and apply to every brain, there are a few that apply more to education than others. Those we talk about coincide with what we previously learned about how the brain learns.

Rule four is that we don't pay attention to things we find boring (Medina, 2008). Keep in mind, however, that our attention is piqued by different things at different ages. The things that a third grader finds interesting are very different from that which a teenager finds interesting, which is different from what an adult finds interesting.

This doesn't mean we need to make Sunday school or Bible Study more entertaining, it means we are interested in things that spark our interest. Our brains pay attention to things with which we have an emotional connection. We like things interesting, meaningful, and/or challenging in some way (Langhoff, 2014). In education we help people of all ages create an emotional connection to the material, but it's done differently for different ages. There will be more on how that works at different ages in later chapters.

Rule five is for short-term memory. We need to repeat to remember (Medina, 2008). Medina says the human brain can only hold about seven pieces of information for less than 30 seconds, but repeating that information will extend that length of time. When somebody gives you some information like their address or phone number and you don't have anything on which to write it down, what do you do? You repeat it to yourself multiple times until you get to a place where you can write it down. This is why the way we have students do memory work doesn't usually work. We have them repeat it multiple times in the fifteen minutes before class and that only puts it in short-term memory.

Rule six is for long-term memory. If you want something to be stored for a long time, it needs to be repeated over time (Medina, 2008). Being exposed to information repeatedly over periods of time helps move information from short to long-term memory. Why? Because when we learn something new our brains create a new synapse and every time that information is referenced in some way that synapse grows deeper or more permanent (Jensen, 2015). It doesn't have to be done immediately or constantly. This is why it helps to ask students what they learned or what was talked about the previous week in Sunday school or Bible study. The best example of how long-term memory works is the liturgy, the Apostles' or Nicene Creed, and the Lord's Prayer, not to mention the hymns we sing over and over again especially during holidays. After repeating these things weekly (or more) for many years we cannot help but have memorized them.

We remember song lyrics we knew in high school when we're much older because of how often we listened to them as teenagers. It's incredibly important for people to get the Bible in their hearts and to do that we need to be sure it gets into their long-term memory at a young age. Repeat and remind every week. The more they are said, the easier it will come back after time.

Rule ten is about vision and how a picture is worth a thousand words. We think in pictures, not words. Even as we read, the brain translates words into mental pictures (Medina, 2008). If I say "ark" people see a number of different pictures of the ark in their minds. If I say the "word ark" we see a picture of the word ark. Our brains don't see words over pictures. The concept of Noah is related to those pictures.

A person will have three times better recall for pictures over words and six times better recall for words accompanied by a visual of some kind (Medina, Vision, 2014). Young children who cannot read learn from pictures, but pictures also help people of all ages remember, especially when teaching about things that students have no prior reference to connect it to. This means that for the most part, if you're lecturing or preaching, slides should contain pictures. For example, when you talk about an altar used in the Old Testament it will be understood better if there's a picture of what it looks like and how it is used. You can imagine that saying Jesus wore a crown of thorns will be remembered much longer if a picture accompanies the words than simply a page of words. Pictures trigger students' recall.

You never want to change too many things about how you teach at once. It can cause stress and may overwhelm you. Change one or two things at a time, get used to them, and then change another. Pretty soon you'll feel comfortable and confident in your new teaching style. Knowing what you do now about how the brain learns and how memory works, take a few minutes to think about how that will affect your teaching. What three to five things would you like to change or add to your Sunday school teaching toolbox or Bible Study facilitation?

Music and Memory

How many of us still sing the Alphabet Song when we need to remember what letter comes before or after another? We recognize songs from our teen years often when we hear the first few chords and the words come flooding back. How many Bible verses do you remember because you learned them in song or rhyme? There are those that we remember due to repetition and those we remember the minute somebody sings the tune. Ephesians 4:32 is one of them for me.

> "Be ye kind, one unto another; tender hearted, forgiving one another; even as God for Christ's sake has forgiven you. Do doo doodely do - Ephesians 4:32."

We remember things far more easily when in song or rhyme. Wallace (1994) found that text is more easily remembered and recalled for both children and adults when it's heard as a song rather than as direct speech. When sung over time the memory will move from short to long term. It was also found that remembering is more effective when the same melody is used for each verse as opposed to different melodies for different verses (Wallace, 1994). As stated before, repetition is the brain's friend.

Music, by its very nature, has a structure that helps learners remember by chunking words and phrases, identifying line lengths, identifying stress patterns, and adding emphasis to certain words or phrases (Wallace, 1994). This is great for memory, but then the question of comprehension comes in. Does memorizing something or being able to easily recall it mean it is comprehended by children? Calvert and Billingsley (1998) would say, no. If the words are not something comprehensible for them in the first place, a song won't make them more-so.

This information also applies to rhymes. While they may make memorization easier, they don't help with comprehension. This indicates the need for prior understanding of or an explanation of the text before teaching the song or rhyme.

Cognitive Development

Cognition is a term psychologists use to refer to the activity of learning to think. A psychologist would call it "the activity of knowing and the mental processes by which human beings acquire and use knowledge to solve problems" (Shaffer & Kipp, 2007). *Cognitive development* is the growth in cognitive abilities (remembering, problem solving, and decision-making) over the course of life. If we watch closely, patterns emerge as people grow and learn.

Jean Piaget (1896-1980), the most influential theorist in the history of child development, began studying development by closely watching his own children interact with others and the world and solve problems. He found that when people have a disparity between their existing knowledge and their external environment, they become curious and intellectual growth occurs. People are constantly organizing and reorganizing what they know and assimilating new experiences into existing knowledge causing learning.

While Piaget was working on his theories, Lev Vygotsky (1896-1934) was also working on his own developmental theories. He believed that a child's cognitive skills were connected to his/her sociocultural context and evolved from social interactions with influential people in his/her life (Shaffer & Kipp, 2007). While both of these psychologists come from different perspectives, their theories are not mutually exclusive.

The stages of learning or milestones of development are not exact. While children develop in the same direction, they progress at their own rate and their sociocultural context plays a huge role in it. People learn when new information is built upon existing information and the guidance and encouragement provided by others makes a difference. This is what makes the Sunday school teacher valuable. What you do changes lives!

Male/Female Brain Distinction

In our current society it may seem like some people want to think there are no differences between males and females, or they're doing everything they can to ignore them. God, however, created men and women differently and those differences go much deeper than appearance, desires, and abilities. Our gender affects our brains and is embedded in us down to our cells (Jensen, 2015).

Sometimes we think little girls are smarter than little boys or we think that little boys are better at math than little girls. While male and female brains are overwhelmingly more alike than different, there are areas where they are different. The biggest difference in both children and adults is that the male brain is about 10% larger in size than the female brain, however, size does not affect learning ability. Overall, there are no gender differences in intelligence between males and females (Jensen, 1998). The research doesn't show that one gender learns better or faster than the other or that males or females are less able to learn certain things, but that different areas of the brain develop in a different sequence, time, and rate. Because of that, and because brains develop during the years children are in school, gender affects how children learn (Sax, 2006).

Kaufmann and Elbel report that in the areas of spatial memory and motor coordination, boys mature about four years earlier than girls (as cited in Bonomo, 2017). Hanlon and colleagues report that in the areas of verbal and written language and fine motor skills, girls develop six years earlier than boys (as cited in Bonomo, 2017). They all get there, but they take different roads on the journey to the same destination.

Due to the uniqueness of every individual, learning is a complex process. The brain structure is not the only influence on learning. There are genetic predispositions, brain sequence and rate of development, individual thoughts and behaviors, individual experiences and the environment in which one lives, and every person's unique body chemistry, especially hormones.

Why is this important for Sunday school? It's important because every class will have both boys and girls in it and when little Johnny can't seem to sit still, but little Susie can, we need to keep in mind that Susie's brain development in a different area is helping her sit still and Johnny's brain is more developed than hers in the area of "throw that ball." If you have male and female fraternal twins you have a boy and girl at the same age growing and learning together. If you read the same book to both children at the same time you may notice that Susie can answer questions about what was read more quickly than Johnny. That may be because Susie's rapid memory retrieval is more developed than is Johnny's. Girls are better at written and verbal language than are boys. That doesn't mean that Johnny cannot do it! It means you should not automatically think Johnny is not as smart as Susie because she is quicker. He will get there! The chart below can help recognize other areas boys and girls are different. As they go through the teen years they start catching up in brain development, but that doesn't mean they get closer to being the same gender. Keep in mind that nothing about the brain is strictly black and white. Many girls may have traits that are recognized as primarily male, and vice versa. These traits are generalized in the chart below.

Girls	Boys
Are more cognitively ready for school than boys at the time and can sit for longer periods.	More interested in being active than passively sitting and learning.
Hippocampus is larger until high school.	Amygdala is larger until high school.
Prefrontal cortex is larger and develops earlier; verbal and written language.	Better early at spatial-mechanical functioning and mathematical reasoning; makes boys like sports.
Have higher serotonin level so make fewer impulsive decisions.	More likely to have attention span and transition problems.
More likely to underestimate their abilities.	More likely to overestimate their abilities.
Prefer cooperative learning.	Prefer competitive learning.
Have the advantage on math facts and arithmetic calculations involving rapid memory retrieval.*	Have the advantage on tests of verbal analogies, which involve mapping relationships in working memory.**
Have the advantage in language production and comprehension.*	Have large advantages on tasks that require transformations in visuospatial working memory.**

In later grades perform better on algebra problems when the cognitive components are similar to those of language processing.*	Excel at tasks that require velocity judgments about moving objects, tracking movement through three-dimensional space, and aiming at a moving or stationary target.**
Adapted from Sax, L. (2006). *(Gallagher, Levin, & Calahan, 2002). **(Willingham & Cole, 1997)	

Keeping in mind that girls' brains develop more in the language area first and boys' in the spatial mechanical area first, the differences in the table below might seem logical.

Girls	Boys
Are more verbal-emotive.	Are more spatial-mechanical.
Can change focus easily.	Focus more on single tasks.
Can explain/describe their feelings.	Have trouble talking about feelings.
Friendships more focused on other girls and conversation.	Friendships more focused on shared interests.
Social hierarchies can destroy a friendship.	Social hierarchies organize relationships and build camaraderie.
Self-revelation is part of friendship.	Self-revelation is to be avoided.
Likely to ask a teacher for help.	May not ask for help.
Want to be with friends when under stress.	Want to be alone when under stress.
Feel uncomfortable when faced with threat or confrontation.	Feel excited when faced with threat or confrontation.
Rarely rough-house for fun.	Often rough-house for fun.
Prefer to read fiction, short stories, and novels.	Prefer nonfiction – real events, action, and how things work.
Anxiety, depression and eating disorders are more common in females.*	Attention Deficit and Hyperactivity Disorder and Operational Defiance Disorder are more common in males.*
Adapted from Gurian, M. & Ballew, A. C. (2003). *However, the difference doesn't occur until puberty.	

Part I:

NARRATIVE STAGE
Preschool through Grade 2

The Narrative Stage consists of the wonderful years when great stories turn into great learning about the God who loves children more than they can imagine. It's the time when these stories become a part of the child's life and world view. Young children become familiar with their God by hearing and learning His stories and there are a lot of them! It's not important that they understand everything about them, it's not important that they can think deeply about them, but it's important that we lay the groundwork and they become familiar with them. It's not only God's story, it's their story. When parents tell a young child that Jesus loves them, they believe it. There are no questions. This person, Jesus, loves them more than anything. He even died for them, whatever that means. They don't understand the concept of death, sins, forgiveness, etc. They only know Jesus loves them and so they love Jesus. Tell the stories of Jesus.

> And calling to him a child, He put him in the midst of them and said, "Truly, I say to you, unless you turn and become like children, you will never enter the kingdom of heaven. -Matthew 18:2-3

Narrative Stage

CHAPTER 2

Preschool

Every age is remarkable, but the younger years are a special time of learning. Their young brains are like little sponges as they learn from everything with which they come in contact. The narrative stage is full of vibrant learning and for preschoolers that means activity.

Emotional and Social

Emotionally, preschoolers are curious explorers. Their lives are full of learning adventures as they joyfully check everything out. Now that preschoolers have learned to talk, they talk about anything and it doesn't have to make sense. Though they are bubbly and talkative, their greater challenge is using words and having the vocabulary to express themselves. They need to be reminded frequently to use their words.

Young children thrive on structure and routine. It gives them security; a sense of well-being and reassurance. They like clear and simple rules and are able to follow through with one or two directions. Redirection works very well with them. They also like to help and like it when they are given jobs like picking up papers or matching colors. They find success with simple directions like:

Can you pick up all the blue papers?

Give everybody one spoon.

Put a crayon on the table in front of every chair.

Preschoolers are friendly, but don't quite understand the concept of friendship. They enjoy being together, but when playing with others they will play next to, but not with others. Playing in groups is not something they understand and you may overhear them trying to decide who the boss is. They learn and practice acceptable limits by pretending someone gets to make the rules. You might also hear them having short conversations with themselves and talking about what they're going to do: "I'm going to play with the babies now." Four-year-olds are imaginative, have a fun sense of humor, and love to exaggerate when expressing themselves. The best thing about preschoolers is that they are spontaneously affectionate. Hug away!

Cognitive

From a cognitive standpoint, preschoolers are taking in everything around them at great speed. Their brains are constantly creating new synapses. They do, however, still struggle with their fine motor skills, which is why we don't expect them to color in the lines and struggle to write letters and numbers. They may hold their pencils or crayons in a fist and while we want them to hold them differently later on, for now, that works fine. Crafts or other projects that require fine motor skills will also be a challenge. It is best to focus more on large movements.

Preschoolers think literally. If you tell them they have ants in their pants, don't be surprised if you see them checking. They also reason according to what things "seem like" to them and their personal experience is limited so their reasoning is often flawed.

If you watch a four-year-old play you can see them learning. You may catch them mimicking their parents as they learn social rules and manners. You may catch them being bossy to someone else, essentially telling them what the rules are. They are learning right and wrong by absorbing everything they see and hear.

Preschoolers can hear and repeat stories, but they may not get things in the right order. They should be able to sort things by shape and size or color, but they cannot yet sort ideas into categories or sequence. At this point in Sunday school they play with the stories and characters in their minds and become familiar with them even though they most likely will not be able to talk about them accurately.

With regard to time, preschoolers have no concept of it other than *now* or *later*, or more precisely, *now* and *not now*. They have no understanding of an hour, tomorrow, next week, or how long class lasts. "Mommy will be coming later." While those phrases may be used often, the concept of time passage is beyond them at the moment.

Behavior

While Sunday school is a short class, preschoolers are very active and don't always know or remember the rules. The best way to teach them the rules for your class is to show them. For example, if you need them to sit on the rug for the story and a few are lying down, show them how you want them to sit. If you want them to put their pencils or crayons in a can, do it while you are telling them. Keep in mind that sometimes in preschool even the simplest rules may not be known. You may not think how a student sits on the rug is a big deal, but many four-year-olds have not been to a formal preschool and have not learned "school" rules or how to behave in a group. Getting these down right away will save you frustration later on.

If you do a standard Sunday school opening you may have students for 30-45 minutes. Here are tips to manage a group of preschoolers.

- Be consistent about sticking to the rules you set.
- Have students help by cleaning up the floor, picking up papers, etc.
- If a student becomes a problem, have him/her be your "helper" and stick by you.
- Give a couple of simple choices whenever possible. For example: you can sit on the rug over here, or over there. Which do you want?
- Use assertive I-messages. Look directly in the eye (assertive discipline) and say, "I need you to…"

Play and Make-Believe

The importance of play for young children cannot be underestimated. It is an integral part of learning in the early years (Gupta, 2009). A huge part of a preschoolers play is pretending. They love to pretend they're mom and dad, fire fighters or policemen, cowboys/girls, super heroes, and princesses. Through stories, role-playing, and make-believe, children are able to express feelings, improve language, and enhance vocabulary (Gupta, 2009).

One of our goals in teaching children about the Bible is to have them repeat stories back to us so that we know they've heard them correctly. Of course, with a preschooler's imagination it may come out very different from the truth as they make the story their own. What we don't want is for them to take incorrect information home or for them to miss the big message about how much God loves them. So, after they've heard the Bible story, provide opportunities for them to tell it back. That's where play comes in. There are multiple ways kids can do this if we provide the right storytelling tools for them. Storytelling tools are toys, puppets, dress-up clothes, props, etc.

I was asked to visit the Sunday school class of a church to give feedback and when I walked into the preschool room I saw a huge piece of cardboard leaning against the wall. My first thought was that it was trash and should be removed, but later on the magic happened. That piece of cardboard became the boat the disciples were in when the storm came up. The teacher read the story and as she did, the kids acted it out, using that piece of cardboard. It became many things.

What things can you do to reinforce the story after you've read it?

- Have children act the story out as you reread it and read it in a way that allows them to act it out. Preschoolers don't work together too well so it works for them to all do it together.
- Have children take turns telling you the story a bit at a time. "Then what happened?"
- Include movement in your stories, for example, sometimes hand motions help children remember what comes next. When the wind and waves come up, so do waving arms.

Knowing that preschoolers use stories and imaginative play to learn, one of the most important things we can do is use stories to teach them about the Bible. For years I've heard people say, "Sunday School is boring for kids because they hear the same stories over and over again." Yes, they do. I do too, and yet every time I read them I learn something new, a truth becomes more solid, and memory of that truth is stronger. What we need to do is make sure we teach deeper as children's brains develop.

A number of years ago I was at the beach with extended family and my cousin's young son, Jimmy, came out one afternoon in his Spider Man clothes. He was covered from head to toe and was jumping from one piece of the furniture to the next using his "webs." One of the adults asked him to stop walking on the furniture and he replied, "I'm not Jimmy!" Preschoolers are serious when they play and use it to learn and practice social rules and behaviors. You may know a little girl who often becomes a princess and behaves like a princess. When they hear stories about different characters they learn how they behave and mimic that later on.

Preschool children have trouble determining what is true and what make-believe is. Jimmy, in his mind, became Spider Man in the same way a little girl becomes a princess. If we tell them Jonah was swallowed by a big fish and Jesus woke up from being dead, they believe it.

Bible Reading

Preschooler children love words. They love rhyming, nonsense words, baby words, animal sounds, made-up words, and even naughty words. They also love being read to and learning songs and rhymes. They can hear the same story 40 or 100 times and sing the same song over and over again.. They have no problem singing songs or Bible verses from memory, especially if they rhyme or have a rhythm to them or have motions. They can even read books to you by the pictures, though the events of the story may not always be accurate.

By the ages of 2 or 3, children begin to develop an awareness of words and printed letters and they start noticing when people around them are reading (Early Childhood-Head Start Task Force, 2002). Preschoolers are especially ready to learn from adults reading to them.

When reading to preschoolers it's important to have a comfortable place for them to sit and to be able to see the pictures. If teachers are excited to share the new Bible story of the week, kids will be excited to hear it. There are a few tips that can help comprehension as you read:

- Have a large rug where children can sit and listen to the stories. Keep in mind that preschoolers are wiggly and have no concept of personal space. It will help to use a piece of masking tape with each child's name on it so they know where they should sit on the rug. Also, they should all be sitting up, listening, and watching. Expect them to pick at the tape. (Masking tape is good because it has a light enough bond not to damage the carpet/rug, but strong enough not to come up too easily.)

- Before you begin reading, introduce the story. "This is a story about a boy named Samuel (1 Samuel 3). God called to him in his sleep. We're going to read about what God said. What do you think God said?"

- Tell the children about the characters before you read the story. Give 2 or 3 options. "Do you think Samuel was excited, frightened, or calm?"

- Pause to explain words they may not know. Be aware that sometimes Bible stories written in rhyme use words above the child's comprehension in order to make the rhyme work. Popular Arch books do this. Check those books before you read them to your class. You don't want to interrupt the story a lot to explain what the words mean and it tells you the book is not appropriate for preschoolers.

- Ask children to point to things in the pictures. "Which one is Samuel? Who are the other people? What do you see in this picture?"

- Ask children to repeat key words or phrases. "When God calls Samuel, Eli tells him to say, 'Speak Lord, your servant is listening.'" Teach students that phrase and have them say it with you when it's spoken in the story.

- Encourage children to identify feelings of people in the Bible stories. "How do you think Samuel felt when he realized God was calling him? How do you think you would feel if you heard God talking to you?"

- Have children tell what has happened in the story so far or ask them what they think will happen next.

- Ask questions that connect the story with the child's life, keeping in mind how literal they are. "When you were baptized you were given to God too and His Spirit lives in your heart."

Every Bible story has a central truth that you want students to take with them. After the story, tell them that central truth and have them repeat it back to you. In the story of Samuel that central truth could encompass the phrase, "Speak Lord, your servant is listening." It could also be Samuel's response to what the Lord told him about Eli and his sons, "It is the Lord. Let Him do what seems good to Him." For a preschooler that message might be: In spite of everything we think we know, *God knows best. We trust Him.* Remember the brain rules for memory. Introduce the phrase when you introduce the story, say it multiple times throughout the story, and end with it. The next week ask them what they learned last week and see if they remember the phrase.

Try to have good children's Bibles with few words and a curriculum that comes with a lot of illustrations. If you can't find one, look online. There are a lot of great pictorial resources out there.

CHAPTER 3

Kindergarten

Kindergarteners are heading across the bridge from preschool into elementary school. They continue to be adorable, have great imaginations, believe what we tell them, and are generally happy.

Emotional and Social

Kindergarten is a time of great overall happiness for children. They have calmed down a bit since preschool, but will continue to struggle with emotional words and may need reminders to use their words to express their feelings and needs. They also love to tell silly jokes. Be sure to laugh!

Five-year-olds experience life through all their senses. They are the center of their universe as they can't imagine how the world looks to other people. They like and want to see, touch, smell, hear, and taste things you wouldn't even consider.

In preschool, children often play next to others, but not necessarily with them. In kindergarten, children learn to play *with* them, but one at a time. Kinders begin to see the benefit of sharing and getting along. They want to be like their friends and want their approval so often will do what their friends do. Five-year-olds become aware of gender differences and are drawn to same-gender friends. They are also beginning to understand empathy and right verses wrong which helps develop friendships. You might also see moments of jealousy if other children spend time with *their* friends.

One of the great things about five-year-olds is their desire to please adults that are significant in their world and be good. They want approval. They accept adult rules as absolute and follow them and may also criticize kids when they catch them not following those rules. Kindergarteners like to volunteer to help and you may hear them ask if it's okay. "Can I do the dishes?" "Can I use these? How many can I use?" "Can I eat this?" "Can I feed the puppy?"

Five-year-olds love attention and will dance, sing, and be silly in order to get it. Enjoy the show, but try to focus all that dramatic energy into having them retell the Bible story.

Cognitive

Kindergarteners are active learners who still primarily think from their point of view. They are the center of their universe and cannot see things from somebody else's point of view. Because of this, they have trouble understanding concepts like *fairness*. They also think literally as opposed to logically. If you tell them that the Holy Spirit ascended like a dove, in their minds the Holy Spirit is a dove. If they see that it gets dark when you turn the lights off, they think somebody turns off the sun and turns on the moon as if it were a night light. "We're late. We've got to fly" may cause them to wonder if they will fly in an airplane or use wings. They use words in their literal sense.

Riding in the car on the way to church one spring day, young sisters, Rachel and Lauren were having a conversation. Older sister, Lauren, made a comment about Jesus being grown up. Rachel, clearly remembering Christmas, told her sister that Jesus was a baby. Lauren responded, "Jesus grew up and died on the cross for our sins." "No, He didn't!" Rachel insisted, "He's a baby!" Lauren tried to explain, "Remember when you were a baby? You grew up? So did Jesus." "NO!" Rachel shouted. Later in church they talked about John the Baptist so in the car on the way home Lauren tried again. She emphasized, "He's the one who baptized Jesus in the river WHEN HE GREW UP!" Rachel is a literal or concrete thinker like most children in kindergarten and was not buying what her sister was selling.

Five-year-olds learn best with structure and routine and like knowing what's coming up. They like to make decisions and giving two or three choices, when possible, is a great opportunity for that. "Do you want to color this picture or that one?" They enjoy sorting and are becoming more attuned to details. As we know from what we learned about the brain in chapter one, repetition is good for learning. In kindergarten, children can easily remember addresses and telephone numbers, songs, poems, and short Bible verses, among other things.

Children in kindergarten enjoy playing matching games and one that can be fun to teach them about the church is to hold up pictures of Christian symbols and have them match pictures (cards) of their own. First try asking them to hold up a cross, then hold up one similar to one that is in their pile of cards and have them match it.

Moving on from preschool, five-year-olds understand the *now* or *later* of time, but still struggle with what "in 5 minutes" or "in a little while" means. They can tell you what will happen and what has happened, but the concept of short or long time passing is still vague. Start talking about time using words like: morning, afternoon, evening, today, tomorrow, yesterday, etc. Sand timers can be helpful because kids can see the time passing, and using phrases like "when the big hand is on the 9 we will say our closing prayer" gives more concrete ways for them to understand the passage or length of time.

Behavior

Kindergarteners are noisy and active, and consistency is the key when it comes to discipline. They respond well to routines and clear expectations. If they have a tendency to interrupt, it's because they are also learning how to take turns speaking and may need some reminders.

Five-year-olds will stretch the truth to test and widen their boundaries and will often try to reason with people using the word "because" a lot. It's not so much to see what they can get away with, but to see what they can do at this age. They appreciate guided choices so they can make some of their own decisions and this works well when something goes awry. It's always easier to tell them what they can do instead of what they cannot do. "You may sit here, or there. Which do you choose?" If you ask them what happened or why they're sitting in the wrong chair, they may give a long elaborate answer.

Once children go to school they will hear language we wish they didn't use. If they talk back or use inappropriate words simply tell them "we don't use those words here" or give a brief time-out and let it go. Making a big deal about it simply makes a big deal about it and gives attention in an area you don't want to give attention.

There are also times when five-year-olds will not get what they want, their emotions will override, and a tantrum will ensue. Don't give them too much attention if this happens. Use assertive I-messages. Look them directly in the eye (assertive discipline) and say, "I need you to…"

Play and Make-Believe

We often push kindergarteners to start reading and "studying" or doing school like older kids because we think that will prepare them for the future, but these early years of play are a very important part of their education. Allow them to be where they are today and teach them where they are today. They are loud and active and love to pretend. They pretend to be mom or dad, astronauts, teachers, animals, Jesus, princesses. As they face bad guys and dragons, pretend to get married, and play with animals on the ark they are learning. As with preschoolers, it's through stories, role-playing, and make-believe that children at this age are able to express feelings, improve language, and enhance vocabulary (Gupta, 2009).

Five-year-olds can tell the difference between what real is and what is make-believe. They give life to inanimate objects so things that may not seem believable in the Bible are easy for them to believe as fact. Along with that, kindergarteners learn best through active play and have very vivid imaginations, which allows them to create very vivid characters that may or may not be real. When my little brother was very young he had trouble sleeping at night because he was sure the lawn mower in his closet would come out and get him. (Of course, he didn't have a lawn mower in his closet.) If you asked him the next day if he was afraid of the lawn mower, he would easily tell you no, but at night when his imagination got going, he was sure that it would.

When teaching kindergarteners, it's good to have props and costumes for storytelling. If you tell students a story, have them tell it back to you using the props and costumes or puppets similarly to when they were in preschool. When you read the story wear a story-telling hat. When they tell the story, have them wear the "story-telling hat."

Books and Stories

Kindergarteners love the pictures in their books and know that stories have a beginning, middle, and end so they will be able to put a story together by the pictures far better than they could last year. They will also be able to identify with the characters. It's important to have good children's Bibles with few words and/or a curriculum that comes with a lot of illustrations. They should be able to recognize the person, place, things, or an idea in an illustration.

When reading Bible stories to kindergarteners, pause to identify key people and point them out to the children. Who do you think this is? Make sure they notice where the story takes place and pause to think about things as you read to model that behavior for the students. Ask them what they think will happen next and don't forget God as the main character that we don't see. Finally, at the end of the story, ask children to share what they liked best and what they want to remember most about the story (Faulk, 2015). If there is a key phrase or verse from the Bible that helps them, make sure they say it with you multiple times so they remember it.

With some help or prompting from the teacher, kindergarteners should be able to answer questions about and retell stories including key details (Faulk, 2015). The things you want to bring out of each Bible story are:

- Characters – people, animals, or things that act out the story.
- Setting – the place where a story happens

- Sequence of events – the order in which things happen in the story.
- Problem/Solution – a situation or event that needs to be resolved in a story. When talking about the Bible one solution is always that God never leaves His people (us too) and always loves them (us).

Before the story begins, give a quick synopsis of what it's about. During the story, pause to ask questions about what's going on in the story and what they predict will happen next, share names, and point things out in the illustrations. After a story, ask questions about what it was about such as:

- Who are the people in the story? (Don't forget God!)
- Where did the story take place? Was it inside or outside? Was it in a building? What building? Was it in the city or country?
- What happened in the story? What did God do in this story?
- What do you think would be a good title for this story?

Kindergarteners can talk about things that have already happened or are going to happen. They can understand what happened last week and you can refer to what will happen in the story this week. Before you begin, make sure you briefly revisit the story from last week, asking students to recall the people and what happened, including what they/you wanted to remember most. Then move on to: "This week our story continues..." Be sure to treat each story as a part of a bigger story, reminding them that this is not only a story about these people, it's a story about a God who wanted to share His love so much that He created people to love Him and when they turned away, He never gave up on them and finally gave His Son for them.

Kindergarteners also like to copy what others are doing, repeat stories, poems, songs, games and enjoy when there's movement to go along with those things. They can hop, skip, and jump as well as using their hands and arms. At this age they do well with directed role-play and dramatic play.

After they have heard the story, some options for them to retell or reinforce the story are:

- Find a way to include movement in the story in the manner of a fingerplay. If people are walking to the Promised Land have students start walking in place. You don't have to write your own, there are books of Bible finger plays! (The Giant Book of Fingerplays for Preschoolers, by Amy Houts)
- Read the story as the narrator and have students speak the dialogue. It will be very entertaining to hear what they come up with!
- Have each child take turns telling you the story a bit at a time. "Then what happened?" It will most likely be broken and out of order.

- Have them tell the story putting the illustrations in the right order. This could be a challenge if your curriculum doesn't come with good illustrations. If necessary, make enlarged photocopies of the pictures in the children's Bible and cut them up.
- Teach them a simplified story in a rhythm so they remember it better. There are books for this, too, but I have not reviewed them. A lot of people like Arch books, but the vocabulary in them is often too advanced for preschoolers.
- Give a student the illustrations and have them "read" it to the class. They will "read by picture" and you'll be able to tell what they got out of it. If the curriculum comes with a paper version of the story with pictures, encourage parents to have the children tell the story after dinner or before they go to bed.

Any time you can turn information into a short song or poem they can speak in rhythm, children will learn it easier.

CHAPTER 4

First Grade

First graders are curious, enthusiastic, imaginative, and fun! They also, if you can imagine, can have trouble staying in their chairs. It's not that they like to get up a lot, but they can and do fall out of their chairs. In first grade students are moving away from a world of play into a world of symbols and understanding those symbols. It is an exciting time!

Emotional and Social

First-graders are noisy and more social than they were last year and first grade classes tend to be noisy and active. They're simply a busy, boisterous, bustling bunch. There's a lot to do and see and learn! In the first grade children enjoy working together on projects or activities, being artistic, and you may overhear them singing, humming, or talking to themselves; some may even whistle as they race through tasks, assignments, and games. They're far more interested in getting to the next task than taking their time with the one at hand.

Children in first grade have a tendency to be competitive and can be bossy and critical of others in that competitive spirit, which can also bring on jealousy of others. They enjoy games and collecting things, including stickers (look at orientaltrading.com for religious stickers) or stamps for doing well or completing a project. In their spirit of competition they can sometimes be poor sports and blame others for something they've done, or change the rules in a game so that they win.

Friends are becoming important in the first grade world and many may have a best friend or many best friends. They enjoy being goofy and performing for others, as well as telling silly jokes, riddles, songs and guessing games. They like working or playing in groups more this year as they learn to interact together and enjoy explaining things and sharing about things they like. First-graders are curious and may also ask a lot of questions.

First-graders are sensitive and accepting criticism is a challenge for them. They thrive on encouragement. Sometimes they have difficulty making decisions and will work more diligently if they work with or next to an adult. They easily become attached to their teachers, are extremely sensitive and anxious to do well.

Cognitive

In first grade logical thought begins to sprout. Children are beginning to be aware of cause and effect. If you don't leave on time you will be late. If you don't watch the ball you may get hit by it. The wind makes the trees move. They are also more comfortable with the idea of past and present. Where kindergarteners may think Adam and Eve live in the garden down the street, first-graders understand that God created Adam and Eve and the garden in the past. Along with that comes the ability to distinguish reality from fantasy.

Unlike kindergarteners, first-graders see other points of view. Until now children think everyone is like them and experience the world the way they do. Now they can consider rules and behavior with greater objectivity.

First-graders love adventure and activities that involve exploration and discovery. They like asking questions, sharing thoughts, and explaining what they know. They are learning to solve problems by trying different things. When looking at pictures they can see how they are similar or different to what they see.

It is in the first grade that children can distinguish their left from their right and consistently track from left to right with their eyes, which makes it a great time to begin learning to read sentences and not merely words.

Behavior

First graders are highly competitive and it shows up in different ways. They may insist on having their own way, may seem frustrated frequently, and may have tantrums when things don't go the way they expect. They often take small things from others and claim they found them. They also may begin to test the limits of authority. Give firm limits and be consistent.

Children in first grade are also excited to do things so much that they rush through things to get to the next thing. Encourage them to slow down and do a good job at whatever they're doing. They enjoy taking on responsibility and can follow through with one or two directions. Helping clean up or pass materials out is a good job for them. Depending on the size of your class you can have a weekly helper or two. Have a place on the wall or the board where you can write down the name of This Week's Helper(s) and Next Week's Helper(s).

At this age children understand that actions have causes and effects, are learning right and wrong, fair and unfair, but without shades of gray. Their thinking is still pretty black and white so try to have simple yes/no rules. They are also learning about speaking politely in a group, waiting their turn and not interrupting. When asking and answering questions, first-graders may need to be reminded of these things.

Play and Make-Believe

In first grade, play continues to be important though it might be more directed in school than at home. Since most first-graders don't read yet, they learn by experiencing or manipulating objects. They count marbles, put things together and take them apart, hear stories, practice manners, learn how to interact with peers and adults, etc. They also enjoy performing for others, pretending, and playing make-believe using costumes and props, though it becomes more elaborate dramatic play than fantasy as they step in and out of reality.

Children in first grade enjoy learning new games and inventing new characters. As in kindergarten, they may even invent new rules or change old ones to suit their desired outcome. First-graders also enjoy crafts, coloring, painting and can cut and paste as they practice fine motor skills.

Books and Stories

Children in first grade love being read to and can listen to stories without interruption. They love books with pictures and should be able to retell the story in proper order with a beginning, middle, end and some key details (who, what, and where). They can reread (or have you reread) a book or story a million times without becoming bored and are beginning to recognize words.

In first grade, children can retell stories with key details (who, where, and what happens) and show that they understand the lesson or moral of the story. One lesson in *every* Bible story is how much God and/or Jesus loves them. Never let kids leave your class without hearing that at least once.

Children can also identify who is telling the story at various points in the text. In Bible stories this can be a challenge because they don't always know who's speaking. One thing we know for sure is that God inspired the whole Bible and it's a story about Him and his people, so He is the author of every story. Sometimes, however, God tells his story through Moses, Matthew, Paul, etc. First-graders may have a hard time with that one.

Six-year-olds like to tell stories from pictures, enjoy "show and tell" and explaining things. This is a good time to start asking WHY something happened or why something is the way it is.

- Why did Noah build the ark?
- Why did Joseph's dad give him the colored coat?
- Why did they put Paul in jail?
- Why does Jesus love you? (Never because you're good. Only because you are God's creation!)

Since they can't read yet, and are still working on fine motor skills, they can't write answers, but children in first grade can use illustrations and details to describe characters, places, what's going on, etc. They can also identify words and phrases in stories or poems that suggest feelings or appeal to the senses.

- Can you tell me what Jerusalem looks like?
- What do you like about it?
- What part of the picture makes you feel like it's a good place?
- Do you think Paul is happy about being in prison? What part of the picture or what words in the story make you think that?
- What words make you think the people love or don't love God?

They can use writing, drawing, speaking, painting, and drama to show thoughts and feelings about a story too.

Try finding ways to include movement into your stories or activities and have different hats, capes, or other props to help them retell stories. Children in first grade enjoy working in groups more than last year, so break them up in groups to retell a story, or if it's a small class, have them work together. After they have heard the story, some options to help them retell for reinforcement are:

- Try having children act the story out as you read it. This doesn't work with every story, but it can be a good way to have kids think about what might be said in certain situations.
- Find a way to include movement in the story or tell the story with hand motions. Sometimes movement helps them remember what comes next. They may remember some fingerplays from previous years.
- Read the story as the narrator and have students speak the dialogue. It will be very entertaining to see what they come up with! "And Jesus said…"
- Have each child take turns telling you the story a bit at a time. "Then what happened?"
- Have them tell the story putting the illustrations in the right order. (If necessary, make photocopies of the pictures in the children's Bible.)
- Teach them the basic story in a rhythm so they remember it better.

- Give a student the book and have him or her "read" it to the class. If the curriculum comes with a paper version of the story with pictures, encourage parents to have their children tell them the story after dinner or before they go to bed.
- As with all children in the narrative stage, any time you can turn information into a short song or poem they can speak in rhythm, children will learn it easier.

If you show them pictures, first-graders should be able to tell the story back to you in the right order (beginning, middle, and end). They enjoy and remember stories and songs with actions. Try having them make up motions and continue repeating them throughout the year. First-graders also enjoy coloring pictures and making simple crafts. In their minds the questions they ask are simple so be sure to answer them simply.

Narrative Stage

CHAPTER 5

Second Grade

Second graders are worriers! They're less impulsive and more serious than they were last year. It's in second grade that children start having an inkling that the world is bigger than they thought and begin to prefer their personal worlds more organized.

Emotional/Social

Second-graders see and feel with thoughtful intensity. Where in first grade they were boisterous and busy, in second grade they may become more quiet, sensitive, self-conscious and self-absorbed; they may appear moody or shy. They are becoming more aware of the details that surround them, including relationships.

In second grade students feel more empathy for others. As they consider others, they think more about themselves and may worry that nobody likes them, needing reassurance that they do. They will typically have one best friend, but that person may change from one to another and back to the first and then to even another. Children in second grade like to work with a variety of partners.

It's during this time that children are learning to filter distractions and focus. They can become engrossed in what they're doing to the point where it may seem that they don't hear what somebody is saying. They work more slowly, like to work alone, or with one partner instead of a group. They also enjoy playing partner games more than large group games. They set high expectations and can be disappointed if their performance doesn't meet that expectation.

Second-graders like their world more organized than previously and prefer parents and teachers who organize. They want to be first, best, perfect. Now that they grasp things like time in schedules, plans, calendars, and rules, they want to get them right. They are sticklers about following directions, are more detail oriented, and like to complete their assignments correctly so much so that they may check in with the teacher to be sure they're doing it right. At this age, children don't like making mistakes and want their work to be perfect.

In second grade, the time when the child's world grows a little bigger and scarier, children like to feel secure and can find that through structure. They enjoy one-on-one conversations, especially with adults. Since they are better able to talk about their feelings, and with their worrisome state, developing a conversational attitude will help them alleviate worry. "How was your day? Are you worried about something?"

Cognitive

In second grade children practice what they've learned so far. They also start understanding other people's points of view. They are becoming more interested in the world around them and can appreciate its beauty and wonder. They like to investigate and enjoy inquiry based activities. They want to know how things work and may take them apart to see if they can put them back together.

At this age, children's listening skills are growing and they can listen and discuss for about 15 minutes. Second-graders like to collect, sort, and classify, and learn better using things they can touch and manipulate. They love to be challenged with projects that include puzzles and games. They are figuring it out! They will love it if you create a way to track the Bible verses they learn or the number of Bible stories they talk about during the year.

Children in second grade are growing an internal sense of time and distance. They can grasp concepts like space and have a growing interest in it. Concepts of fairness can be discussed as second-graders have a growing sense of justice.

Play

For second-graders, play takes a new form. They've left a lot of fantasy behind, though they still enjoy drama, memorizing poems and songs, and like making up and saying chants and cheers.

When you're seven years old you're driven by curiosity and a desire to discover and invent. They may create forts, build tree houses, enjoy secret codes, Morse code, pig Latin, etc. Legos and other building toys become popular as do building imaginary play houses and making crafts. Second-graders are explorers! Their play is about fun and thinking.

Behavior

Second graders need stability and predictability, consistent schedules, and routines. They are bothered by their mistakes and become quiet and sullen when angry. Children this age have not learned to lose games and may cheat or end the game abruptly if they're not winning.

Eight-year-olds listen well. They work hard, like doing things right and their work to be correct, and want to finish what they start. Kids this age want to please others and are sensitive to blame. They don't like to be singled out or be the center of attention. If they need correction, try a one-on-one conversation first. If necessary, have them sit down away from the class to calm down. Second-graders are sensitive little people.

Reading and Stories

Second-graders still love being read to, but are starting to read with fluency. They're becoming more interested in chapter books than picture books. They can retell stories and determine their central message or lesson, acknowledge differences in the points of view of characters and may even speak in different voices for each character when reading aloud. This would be a great opportunity to have students read aloud if they're reading a children's Bible at their reading level.

Children at this age retell stories with key details and will ask and can answer who, what, where, when, why, and how questions. They also love words and the meaning of words. This would be a great time to have a word wall for new Bible words and theology terms. Second-graders will be able to have greater understanding of concepts like forgiveness and sinfulness. Having them on the wall will be a good reminder to talk about their meanings. Puns and word jokes will also be popular.

In second grade, children can ask and answer questions such as who, what, when, where, why, and how to demonstrate understanding of a story. When reading to second-graders, be sure to continue to pause to ask questions. If the story of the day is about Peter denying Jesus three times (Mark 14:66-72, Luke 22:54-62, John 18:15-18, 25-27), a few questions might be:

- Who was with Peter?
- What did the rooster crowing mean?
- Where did this happen?
- How did the accusers know Peter was with Jesus?
- How does this story make you feel?
- Why do you think Peter denied that he knew Jesus?
- What can we learn from this story?

Children can also describe how characters in a story respond to major events and challenges. Things were getting tougher for Jesus. How were the people responding to him? How did Peter respond to the people? Was he sad, angry, or worried? How do you think he felt? How does the story begin and end? Do you think Jesus was sad that Peter denied Him? What is happy about this story?

Second-graders can identify with Bible characters. Some strategies from first grade will also work with second graders though they will have deeper understanding and more accurate retelling. Keeping in mind that second-graders prefer to work solo or with one partner, after they have heard the story and answered the questions, some options for them for retelling or reinforcement are:

- Have children create paper puppets and tell the story to each other. One can start and the other can end.

- Have students retell the story and continue to include movement and have costumes and props.

- Read the story as the narrator and have students speak the dialogue. It will be very entertaining to see what they come up with! "And Jesus said…"

- Have each child take turns telling you the story a bit at a time. "Then what happened?" Let the next child continue.

- Have them tell the story as they put illustrations in the right order. (If necessary, make photocopies of the pictures in the children's Bible.)

- Teach them the basic story in a rhythm so they remember it better.

- Any time you can turn information into a short song or poem they can speak in rhythm, children will learn it easier.

- Sit in a circle and have students use facts from the story to answer questions. For example, what did the people say to Peter? (Children can work with partners to look in the book and see what was said.)

- Break the story verses into parts or chunks and have children put them together in the right order.

CHAPTER 6

Story Telling

For centuries people had no written Bibles to read and so shared the stories of Abraham, Noah, Samson, and the rest by telling them generation after generation at home, in the market squares, as they worked and traveled and lived. Telling stories and talking about them is a fantastic tool for teaching young people about the Bible and its author. Yes, they can read the stories themselves or have them read to them. They can watch cartoons and movies about them, but what a greater impact they will have if parents tell them on their way to school or on a road trip. What a greater impact they would be if they were stories we talked about in regular daily life and not solely on Sunday morning. How much more impactful is it when a family talks together about their great God and what He has done for them. "You know, there was a man/woman in the Bible who was like that." It becomes people communicating, families bonding, communities growing. Also, passing on a story orally requires the ability to know it well enough to share it, and the process of retelling a story solidifies it in the memory.

Whether in Sunday school or at home, we need to make these stories a part of our lives; we need to make the people of the Bible our ancestors, not only characters in a book. They *were* the people of God. We *are* the people of God. Here are the basics for how to use storytelling in a Bible study, for a children's message, or anywhere. First, don't let people have Bibles open so that they listen and pay attention.

Storytelling Tips

It's not about telling a story, it's about telling a *compelling* story, and the stories in the Bible are compelling and are about a great God who is mighty and awesome and loving beyond our comprehension!

It is the story of an epic struggle between good and evil as darkness tries to eliminate the light. It is the story of a people who got themselves in

43

trouble over and over and a God who rescued them in spite of the fact that they did not deserve to be rescued. There is corruption, intrigue, conflict, suspense, and love, forgiveness, and grace. It is the greatest rescue story ever known to mankind and the people in it are interesting, passionate, caring, and failures, the same way we are. It is our story as much as theirs. Tell that story!

1. Pray that God be with you as you take His story and share it with others. Pray that He enlighten you and bring to your mind His desires. Pray that He speak through you.

2. Read the story **aloud** several times over a period of time. Read it until you can write down the sequence of events without looking at the Bible. Sometimes it helps to read it in different translations.

3. Read the chapters around the story to get a good idea of it in a broader context. Make sure when you tell it to children that the vocabulary is understandable.

4. Ask God to help you discover the point of the story that He wants you to tell and the amazingness of it.

5. Put the book aside and tell the story. Practice it a few times and then record it to check for tone, inflection, etc. (Be sure to keep God's Word separate from any personal interpretation you might have.)

6. It's truth. Do your best to make it come alive!

If you're in Sunday school you tell the story once and then have children tell it with your help. If it's a small class people can volunteer to tell it, they can tell it to each other, or you can start and have different people continue it until the end. Don't be afraid to stop and correct or add details if the story becomes distorted or if important items are left out. God's story is exciting enough without us embellishing it. Be sure to ask questions after the story. Check in the appropriate chapter for age-appropriate questions.

Echo Story

Oftentimes we use echo prayers when we pray with children because they are simple, they use words that the kids can understand, and they help children learn to pray and feel more comfortable praying out loud. The leader says a *short* phrase and the kids repeat it. These prayers are short and to the point.

Developmentally, younger kids *love* stories. They learn from a story far more than a stand-alone message that somebody tells them from an unattached scripture passage. They simply don't connect things as much as we may think they do. Echo stories can be used both in a Sunday school lesson and/or for a children's message.

An Echo Story is when you have specific places within the story where the kids will repeat a phrase, or answer an echo question. You can write your own version or use a good children's Bible and adjust it as needed. You'll need to create a signal of some kind so the kids know when to repeat. You can point at them, have a stop/go sign, put your hand to your ear, etc. You can also put the words up on a screen, if you have one, but remember how many children in the class or children's message can't read.

Here's how it works.

Question Echo – While you share the story, pause to ask simple questions.

> "One day a man named Jonah was told by God to go somewhere. Who was the man? JONAH! Who told him to go? GOD! God told him to go to the city called Ninevah because the people were bad. What was the name of the city? NINEVAH! How were the people being? BAD

You don't need to ask a question after every single point but you do want to make sure the kids repeat the important parts of the story as that's what they'll remember most.

Pause to Repeat Echo – While you share the story, pause specific places to have the kids repeat that line.

> "Zacchaeus was a short, rich man. He took money from people to give to the government so *nobody liked Zacchaeus*. NOBODY LIKED ZACCHAEUS. He wanted to see Jesus. Hmmm, what should Zacchaeus do? He looked around at all the trees around him and *climbed up a tree to see Jesus*. HE CLIMBED UP A TREE TO SEE JESUS."

You'll want to make sure these are pretty short and that the lines are kept short enough that the kids can remember them. You also want to remember that you're telling the story to get a point across so you need to make sure you have them repeat the parts that make your point.

Repeat the Phrase Echo – Tell kids that every time you put your hand to your ear they should echo a specific phrase, or every time you say certain words they echo a specific phrase back to you. For example, if the basic message is JESUS LOVES EVERYONE you can tell a story about a bunch of mean, sad, ugly, unexpected types of people.

> One day a bunch of people went to the Ugly Zoo. At the Ugly Zoo there were a bunch of uglies. The group started down the hall and stopped at the first window. At the top was a sign that said: **Mean Words**. Inside there was a girl saying all kinds of mean things to the people as they walked by. "You're ugly," she would shout at

one person. "You're stupid," she would shout at another. JESUS LOVES EVERYONE! The next window had a sign that said: **Pusher**, because he was always pushing everybody around. "Do it my way," he would say. JESUS LOVES EVERYONE! The sign above the next room said, **Crabby**. As people walked by she complained about everything. "I don't like this food," she said. "I want a new dress!" JESUS LOVES EVERYONE! And so on to visit angry, sloppy, grumpy, pride, hit her brother, stole a cookie, or whatever suits the need. Everybody has a bad day and everybody gets in a bad mood, but thanks to God, JESUS LOVES EVERYONE!

If there's a specific Bible passage you'd like them to remember, make it short and have them repeat it after you a few times throughout the story similarly to Repeat the Phrase.

CHAPTER 7

Children's Messages

The Children's Message, Lamb's Lesson, Children's Sermon, or whatever name it's called at your church, is the time in the service when the children go up to the front of the sanctuary and somebody gives them information. Before talking about crafting a children's message there are a few questions that need to be addressed:

- What is the purpose of a children's message?
- To whom is the message addressed?
- What ages are the children who come up to hear the message?

Hopefully the purpose is to leave younger children with a nugget of God's truth and a reminder that they are loved independent of their behavior. If that is the purpose then the message is addressed to children; usually children from preschool through about second grade. A few older children may come up and a few parents may bring younger children up to get them used to the process, but the message is focused on those in the narrative stage: preschool through second grade.

About Children's Messages

First, let's talk about the children's message. People have been putting them in worship services for many years with the goal of bringing a simpler message to the children who will not get much out of the sermon due to their limited cognitive abilities.

I have seen many messages in my years. Most of them were an attempt at a clever object lesson trying to explain complex theology or Bible concepts to young children. Usually the congregation loves them, however, the children don't get them. For example: At one church there was one lady who always gave the children's message on Christmas day. People raved about it. Every year she pulled an elaborate Rube Goldberg type of toy into the sanctuary and the children oohed and aahed over it. She would put a marble in it and it would go through all these tubes and drops and spins as it made its way to the bottom. She would then talk to the children about life's challenges and how Jesus was born to save us from our sins and help us through life's challenges. My question: What does a kindergartener understand about life's challenges? How does a preschooler connect that cool toy to their life? They can't. For the kids, that children's message was all about watching the cool toy and had nothing to do with Jesus.

I've seen people try to explain the trinity with an apple, a hardened sinful heart with a Tootsie Pop, and the Holy Spirit with a balloon to children who cannot transfer the concept (that they cannot understand) to any object no matter how clever it seems to an adult.

The truth is that the majority of children's object lessons aren't for the kids if the kids are under eight years old. In the early elementary years faith takes the form of story or drama which means the young kids who come up to the front of the church for your object lesson don't have the ability to connect the object to your intended concept. It's a higher order thinking skill. Their young brains simply can't get it.

Cognitive Development of Kids 2nd Grade and Below (Ages 3-7)

Look back at the developmental levels in the previous chapters. The younger they are the more concrete or literal they think. When they are told that the Holy Spirit ascended LIKE a dove, children understand that the Holy Spirit IS a dove. They learn through experience at this age and they know what a bird is. These little lambs:

- Have little ability to think in terms of general principles (kindness, goodness, sin, forgiveness, etc.)
- Have little ability to think about non-physical entities (God, heaven, etc.) God the father is a really big dad. Heaven is an actual place like the library or a big park.
- Have little ability to understand symbolic meaning. Visual symbols do not initially have symbolic meaning -- children must be taught what the cross means as a symbol.
- Cannot relate one fact to another, for example, the heart being like the inside of a tootsie pop that was hardened on the outside by sin. No way.
- Cannot make generalizations like what happens to a Sunday school class when the word of God is shared. If they can't see it happen, super no way.
- Classify Bible stories as any other stories. There is none more or less important. Jonah and Pinocchio are on the same level of truth or make-believe. They start coming out of this in second grade.

- Primarily perceive miracles in the same way as fairy tales. They cannot understand them as real or fantasy. Again, they start coming out of this in second grade.
- Determine the difference between real and make believe better as they age, but that's different than taking something that sounds like it can't be real (coming back from the dead) and assuming it's real.
- Do not understand metaphors. Their literal thought would believe a hardened heart actually gets hard like a rock and Jesus lives in a tiny room in their heart.

For example, one Sunday the sermon was called *Rejected!* It was based on Luke 4:16-31, specifically verse 24, "Truly I tell you," He continued, "No prophet is accepted in his hometown." The person giving the children's message started telling the kids a story about how somebody got a letter of rejection from Harvard University. First of all, children 3-7 years old have no understanding of rejection and it would be a challenge to explain it to them as they have no experience with it. Second, they have no idea what Harvard University or a letter of rejection is. He might as well have been speaking to them in Chinese. He asked questions they couldn't possibly answer and finally let them go. This was a non-object object lesson.

If the majority of children in your congregation who come up for the children's message are seven or younger and you're doing object lessons, you might want to change it up if your goal is for them to take a nugget of God's truth and love with them.

A Meaningful Children's Message

If the majority of the kids who come up during your children's message are younger than 7 or 8 there are things you can do if you want the message to be for them and you want it to be meaningful.

- Remember the brain rules. If you want children to remember something, it needs to be repeated. Try connecting one message to the next with a quick review question. There's a week in between lessons, so there won't be much memory if you don't make it intentionally memorable.
- Remember that a child's life is much simpler than ours. They do not understand life being hard, difficult, or challenging. The vocabulary you use is important. It's also not a good idea to make your messages about being good. This happens often. Jesus doesn't love them because they're good.
- A child repeating a correct answer doesn't mean he/she has understanding. "Children can learn the technical verbal symbols of theology and use all of the proper terms and still not be able to define or apply those terms to everyday life" (Hendricks, 1980).

While we want children to understand, there is nothing wrong with getting them familiar with terms before they understand their full meaning.

- Young children love stories like Narnia, but they do not connect Aslan to Jesus. They love Aslan. If you tell a story to try to get them to understand another point, they will most likely miss it. A story about a little girl who gets a gift is simply a little girl who gets a gift. They will not connect that to grace as a gift, even if you're very direct about saying that. They will, however, connect that story to a time when they got a gift.

Now we know that what we've been doing for years doesn't work and why, if our goal is to share a nugget of God's truth and have children take it with them. It's time to make a change, but what works?

What Works

Our greatest desire is for children to know that God loves them more than they can imagine and after that, to become familiar with Him, and His people, of which they are one. We want them to know that they are part of a family of believers. We do not need to try and explain life to them. They will experience it as they grow. We do not need to find clever ways to try and explain things they cannot understand. We can tell them that God is so amazing and cool that there are mysteries that only He knows. The Trinity is three people, but one person. What? How can that be? There is no possible way to explain it, especially to young concrete thinkers. Don't tell them it's an apple (seeds, fruit, skin) or water (solid, liquid, ice). They can't imagine that anyway and it's not actually true. The Trinity is not three different parts that make up a whole. It/they are three and one at the same time; always.

When you are creating a children's message, before you look for cute or clever ideas, decide on your goal. What do you want the children to leave believing? I use the form below. If the pastor's message is about Jesus going back to Nazareth and being unwelcome, you could briefly tell the story and use pictures on the screen. If you don't have a screen you should print pictures. You can easily find pictures online or look for a good children's Bible. Little kids don't know what it means to be rejected or to go somewhere and be unwelcome. They certainly don't understand the concept of a prophet being rejected in his hometown and what that's all about. So, what's your goal? What, out of that story, can they understand? What the pastor talks about won't necessarily be what the children's message can be about, and everything can't be about how somebody was treated and how that makes them feel. Here's a suggestion:

Title: Jesus Unwelcome in Nazareth	
Scripture	Luke 4:24
Pastor's Theme or Sermon Title	Rejection! Luke 4:16-31
Take Away	Jesus loves us even when we're mean or don't believe.
Handout	None (I'm not handing anything out for them to keep. Sometimes I give stickers or bookmarks or something similar.)
Scriptural Focus	Jesus was rejected in his hometown. His friends and family didn't believe him.
Aids (pics, props, etc.)	The congregation says things like, "You're Mary and Joseph's son! You're a carpenter, not a prophet! When did you get so smart? Who do you think you are?"
Message: In the Gospel lesson today we heard the story of when Jesus went home to Nazareth to visit. He was a little boy there and grew up in the same way you're growing up here. He lived there and played with friends there. He was Jesus, the carpenter's son. Nobody knew He was God's son except Mary, Joseph, and him. So, when He came back as a prophet (a guy who delivers messages from God) the people didn't believe him. They said, (congregation says phrases above). Do you think Jesus stopped loving them when they were mean like that and didn't believe him? No! He didn't! If you were there what would you want to tell them? I would say this; repeat it after me, "Jesus loves you! Jesus loves me! Even when we're mean or don't believe!" (Say it in rhythm multiple times.) Then, have them teach it to the congregation. That's the thing with Jesus. He loves us no matter what! Always!	
Echo Prayer	Dear Jesus, Thank you for loving us even when we do mean things, push you away and forget that you always tell us the truth. In Jesus' name, Amen

There are a lot of options besides object lessons. To illustrate that the message is more important than who gives it, one presenter had a few children read something simple written for them. Then those little ones who couldn't read were taught by them to repeat it and following that the little ones taught the congregation to repeat it. A Director of Christian Education at my church used the congregation to tell the story of Jesus calming the storm. The congregation started making storm noises and waving their arms like waves and the children were Jesus. As the children walked down the aisle the storm grew until they shouted, "Stop!" Jesus has power over nature. Other options are:

- Tell stories that are close to the emotions of the child. Stories that use human characteristics such as loving, sharing, and caring are excellent at this age.

- Use poems, riddles, and songs. Putting scripture to rhythm and song helps them remember it. They need to be short, so break a verse down into a memorable phrase and have them repeat it multiple times throughout your message.

- Use illustrations. Children read picture books and we know from Brain Rules that pictures help us understand and remember. If you're telling a story make sure you use illustrations.

- Use props, pictures, voices, puppets, and/or volunteer actors to tell stories.

- If you have an abstract moral they won't get it, but they can answer simple questions like, "What happened when I...?" "What happened when (the puppet) hit the other one?" "What would happen if you...?" The information needs to be relevant to their experience, which is very much about them (egocentric).

- Show pictures on the big screen and have kids answer questions about the picture. "What's happening in this picture?"

- Teach them what Christian symbols stand for by showing pictures and repeating names.

- Add movement to a story you're telling. Teach them the stories of the Old Testament with hand motions. Add one a week and by the end of the year they'll be able to tell the whole thing!

- Have a repeated or repeatable phrase or Bible verse. Repeat it throughout. Use an Echo Story technique.

There are any number of things other than an object lesson that can be done more effectively for a children's message. The key to the whole thing is to focus the message on the developmental level of the majority of the children who participate. Have fun!

Part II

KNOWLEDGE STAGE
Grade 3 through Grade 5

The Knowledge Stage is the upper elementary years when children learn more about God's stories. It is the time of learning more detailed Biblical facts of the stories and talking about them, laying the groundwork for advanced study. Children at this age are seeing a bigger, more complex world and have questions. Who are the disciples and what was their purpose? How did people live then? Who is Noah and what can we learn from his story? Where did Paul go on his journeys and what happened to him? They start asking who God is, why Jesus died for us, and who or what the Holy Spirit is. Going over the same stories they learned about when in the narrative stage, students see them as bigger and more complex than they were before and begin to understand more of the details as their world grows. As upper elementary children continue to grow they will understand more about sin, death, and the resurrection. They are growing in knowledge and with that comes curiosity and questions. This is the beginning of Bible Inquiry.

So faith comes from hearing, and hearing through the word of Christ. Romans 10:17 ESV

Knowledge Stage

CHAPTER 8

Third Grade

Children in third grade are full of adventure, curiosity, imagination, and positive energy. It's in the third grade that children begin to become curious about other people and how they live. Last year they were realizing that the world was bigger than they thought and this year they're seeing social issues and wanting to do something about them. It's a time of understanding and action.

Social and Emotional

Talkative and social, eight-year-olds used last year's reflection time to grow in confidence and competence and now love to compare and compete. They are cheerful and love to share humor and enjoy riddles, rhymes, silly jokes, and will actively seek praise.

Being more social than last year, third-graders work and play well in groups so cooperative work and group activities and projects are well-received by them, though they interact better when a teacher assigns who is in the group. They're starting to understand what it means to work as a team and learning to cope with change and problem solving.

With all the enthusiasm and excitement of taking on an exciting project, they are full of ideas, big ideas, and are likely to become frustrated when they take on more than they can accomplish in a reasonable amount of time, which they often do. When this happens they may break down and bit and need parent and teacher encouragement and appreciation.

Where in second grade students were very concerned with accuracy, in third grade children will choose speed over accuracy so they can get more done. Third-graders bounce back quickly from mistakes or disappointments and if they find something challenging complaints of "I'm bored!" may be heard.

Eight-year-olds are ready to make new friends though they may lack skills to build relationships. They tend to exaggerate and may tell private information. Generally they have same gendered friends and want peer approval as much as the teacher's.

Third-graders are beginning to think about how others see them and begin to define themselves based on attributes and achievements, such as "I wear glasses." "I play soccer." "I won the spelling bee so I'm good at spelling." They can also become self-conscious based on how they believe they look in the eyes of others. The teenage years are not so far away.

In third grade children are competitive and, as I mentioned before, like to get things done quickly. Along with that, they like to keep track of their accomplishments. They may keep track of how many math facts they remember, how many books they've read, who can run the fastest, etc. This would be a great time to see how many Bible verses they can not only memorize, but remember from week to week.

Third-graders have a growing sense of moral responsibility and interest in fairness. You may hear, "It's not fair!" more than last year, but they're also becoming aware of unfair behaviors or social issues beyond themselves. They will enjoy activities that build a sense of unity and would enjoy working together on a couple of service events each year.

Cognitive

Third-graders learn best through active, concrete experiences, but as they become better readers, they see books as sources of information. In third grade reading may be of greater interest.

While in third grade children can reason logically, it's primarily about objects (how small engines or an instrument works) or real experiences (learning how to win at tic-tac-toe) and not ideas. Their abstract reasoning abilities are very simple and relate to real experiences.

In practicing their logical reasoning, eight-year-olds enjoy collecting, organizing, and classifying objects and information, which leads to learning to plan ahead and evaluate what they do. Keep in mind that enjoying organizing doesn't mean it will be done correctly or consistently. They show increasing interest in rules, logic, how things are put together, how things work, the natural world, and classification. They make choices based on what they want to do and don't necessarily think through how they will do it. Third-graders have increased problem-solving skills and are curious about magic tricks. "How do they do that?"

Third-graders are beginning to see and understand other people's perspectives. They see things through the eyes of others more than last year, but they still see things more concretely than abstractly. For them, things are right or wrong, wonderful or terrible, with little middle ground.

Behavior

Third-graders are becoming more confident and may have a know-it-all attitude. They may also have a bit of a sharp tongue, exaggerate, and share inappropriate information. They are sensitive to criticism, especially in front of others. More than last year, they may question authority and test limits, saying, "That's dumb," or "I don't want to do that," when suggestions are made. When that happens stay positive. "You may find it more fun than you think. Give it a try."

Eight-year-olds are interested in rules and rituals and enjoy consistency, though overall they adjust well to change. The also tend to be sloppy, can be impatient, and may be selfish and demand attention. They are learning how to lose and need to be reminded to lose gracefully. You may see some frustration when things they plan don't work out.

Bible Reading

Third-graders are reading with better fluency and their vocabulary is growing rapidly. They enjoy humor in stories as well as life, which can be a challenge when reading the Bible as we've been trained not to see any humor in Bible stories. We've also been trained to read it without any inflection. It's time to frame it differently. Perhaps thanks to movies like *The Ten Commandments*, God only speaks in a loud, booming voice and Jesus with a soft, reverent, emotionless voice. Apparently one can't be perfect and have a sense of humor, though I'm sure He did as much as we do.

Using the story of David and Goliath (I Samuel 17) for the examples, when it comes to reading, third-graders should be able to:

- Use the story itself to answer questions. For example: How did Goliath taunt David? They should be able to refer to the story and share exactly what Goliath said or did.
- Retell the story accurately.
- Determine the central message, lesson, or moral. For example: What can we learn from the story of David and Goliath? Children should be able to infer that they should trust in God and not themselves, that God is there when they do something in His name, and/or other lessons.
- Describe the characters in a story (e.g., their traits, motivations, or feelings) and explain how their actions contribute to the sequence of events. Try writing the names of all the characters in the story on a card and have students tell each other their purpose in the story. How did they contribute? They can use the cards then to tell what each one did in the story. For example: Saul – couldn't find any of his soldiers to fight Goliath.

- Tell the story from their own point of view as the narrator or as one of the characters. Have children tell the story as if they were there witnessing it. How would David tell the same story?

- Talk about how the story makes them feel about the characters and the situation. What do they think the mood of the story is and how do they think Saul felt when young David volunteered?

- Describe the kind of person David was (and other characters) and how he's like them or different from them. How many of them would do what David did?

Tips to Help When Reading

Sometimes third-graders have difficulty reading. They still need a lot of practice and can omit words or read words out of order. They may also prefer silent reading and that may be encouraged at home. In Sunday school you can encourage, but don't need to force children to read out loud. Also, at third grade all children should have a Bible of their own to read at home. Encourage parents to allow children to read to them as much as they read to their children.

New Words – Illustrations are still very valuable tools to help third-graders understand what they're reading and analyze the text. If they get stuck have them look at an illustration and see if that helps. They can also use context; asking what's going on in the sentence or paragraph to help figure out the meaning of the word. Phonics or sounding out the word by the sounds the letters or groups of letters make can be helpful in reading some words, but doesn't help with word meanings unless they know root words, prefixes, and/or suffixes.

Thoughtful Pause – Have students stop to talk about what was read in the last paragraph. It is a good tool to help children understand what has just been read.

New Words – There are a number of words (people and places) in the Bible that are difficult to read. Few of us know how to pronounce them. We don't know Greek or Hebrew syllables or emphasis. Make sure they know that and allow them to pronounce them however they make sense. Encourage them to pronounce the few common words that we pronounce in a particular way in that way, but make sure they understand that unless we have studied Greek and Hebrew, we're all guessing.

Word Wall – Write or print new words on large pieces of paper. Create three sections: regular words, places, and names. As you come across new words, add them to the wall and every week take about five minutes to go over the definitions of the regular words so students don't forget. If you want to teach them, separate the regular words into parts of speech. What is *steadfast* love? What does it mean to search *diligently*? What is *frankincense* and *myrrh*? If you use a children's Bible or a Bible that is written for children their age it will be a lot easier and they won't be overwhelmed by the vocabulary. Also, while a lot of people love Arch books words that rhyme are often chosen over words that are age appropriate.

Tips for Teaching Third Grade

Some of the tips for second grade will also work with third grade. Based on what we know about third-graders, here are some ideas:

- Enjoy their sense of humor, jokes, riddles, etc. Let go and laugh with them!
- Encourage them to do good work and not only fast work.
- Create a chart to keep track of Bible verses learned. Midway through the year and at the end of the year have parents in and let the kids say the verses to them as a group.
- With budding social interest, allow them to participate in servant activities both inside and outside the church. Is there a group in the wider community to which they would like to donate their offering?
- They like to talk and socialize so find more ways to let them work with mixed gender groups.
- Let them tell each other what they thought of a story or idea.
- When reading the Bible, use their developing sense of logic to make sense of the story. Perhaps break the parts of the story apart in strips and have them logically put the pieces together. Use illustrations to help them tell the story in small groups with each person taking a character.
- Allow them to draw pictures of their thinking. They find learning about other people interesting so talk not only about the characters of the Bible but also of their cultures.
- Third-graders enjoy imaginative play. Let them put on skits or puppet shows to show what they've learned from a story, or the story itself.
- Do projects that spur interest in reading and research, especially the culture. Pose some questions on a worksheet and let children work in groups to use the Bible to answer them.
- In groups, have students write the major points of story on letter paper, mix them up and have each member of the group choose one and put it in its correct place in the sequence of events. When they're done, have the rest of the class check it. If it is correct, the group should then retell the story to the whole class.

Knowledge Stage

CHAPTER 9

Fourth Grade

Fourth-graders are a mix of excitement and anxiety. They are impatient so learn best when the teacher remains calm. As their world view continues to grow and social issues become more complex, they think more deeply about them and want to do what they can to make things better.

Social and Emotional

In fourth grade each child's individual personality and way of presenting him/herself to the world becomes clearer. They are at the very beginning of clarifying who they are as unique individuals. Because of that and their growing world-view, they have a bit of an uneasy approach to life. Fourth-graders become more concerned about global justice and start asking questions like: Why are some people poor? Why are some people cruel to animals? Why is there evil in the world?

Peers have ever greater importance and fourth-graders now pay attention to social groups. Cliques may develop. They can tell you who's in and who's out. At this age fairness matters a great deal and they have a greater sense of group solidarity. Fourth-graders will often speak as a group when they claim something is not fair or that they "never get to do anything."

The moods and interests in fourth grade may shift quickly. They may become distant and aloof or negative one minute and goofy, fun, and caring the next. Children are trying harder to be unique and fit in at the same time and may try out different styles and personalities. They can be very critical of themselves and others. When things become challenging or repetitious you may hear them say, "This is boring," or "I hate this!" Some of these moments can be alleviated by giving very clear instructions before work begins.

While they can work well in groups or teams, fourth-graders are very competitive in classwork and in sports and may argue when working in groups. They would prefer working with a partner of their choice which is good for many Sunday school tasks.

In fourth grade children will sometimes complain and exaggerate physical or growing pains and need adults to make light of the drama. Recognize and validate their feelings of frustration and give them the tools to cope without allowing the drama to take over. If adults have a sense of humor and can make light of what the child is going through, using positive language and encouragement, the student will lighten up more quickly.

Cognitive

Fourth-graders still have trouble understanding abstract concepts though they have an understanding of time as it relates to the past, present, future, today, in five minutes, next week, etc. There are a few things that change in children during fourth grade that affect how they interact with the world. They become more logical, their world view grows, and they have a greater ability for independent thought. They:

- Become deeply aware of the complexities and subtleties of the world around them.
- Like to negotiate, though their logic will be faulty.
- Begin to understand ethical and moral behavior at a new level.
- Grow in intellectual curiosity.

In fourth grade children have a greater understanding of how the world operates. They see that things are complicated and yet see solutions that are simple. They question choices adults have made in the world and feel the desire to affect change.

At this age children focus on the real world and are industrious, and less imaginative than last year, but are more curious and want to explore ideas. They are looking for the reasons why things work or why things happen the way they do, especially around issues of fairness and justice. You may hear, "Why do we have to do this?" on occasion.

Behavior

Children in fourth grade can be moody and critical of themselves and others. They may have hurt feelings and bite fingernails or twist their hair to relieve stress and often complain that things aren't fair. Don't make those incidents more important than they are. If you make fourth-grade drama the focus of your class, it will be the focus of your class. Listen, encourage, and move on.

Fourth-graders may say what they think without thinking first and they enjoy commenting on what's going on. This may require some reminders of manners, how to interact appropriately in discussion, and to think before you speak.

Since fourth-graders are becoming more logical and like to negotiate, when they find themselves in trouble they may try to negotiate their way out of it. Be a smart negotiator and give options: "You can either work together or you can work with me."

If students tell inappropriate jokes or unthinkingly write on tables, it is important to remind them of what is appropriate behavior and have them clean up their graffiti.

Bible Reading

Fourth grade is a good time to focus on comprehension and interpretation when reading and begin research tasks. Fourth graders enjoy language and words, especially descriptive language, word play, and new vocabulary; short dramatic skits or role-plays are also popular and a good way for them to get comfortable with a reading.

This means fourth grade is a good time to start talking about terms used in doctrine and Bible terms. Teach them both what they mean and where they come from. Try doing a word study with them once in a while so they learn how to study passages with words they don't understand. This is a good time to introduce a concordance and Bible dictionary as well so they become comfortable using them.

Fourth graders can read to learn which takes reading the Bible to a new level. They can look back and refer to details and find examples in a text when answering questions. They can infer with better reason why something might be said or done, for example: What might happen if Noah let other people into the ark?

When reading the Bible stories with them, be sure to ask questions that have them refer to details in the text and expect them to use them when answering questions. It's important for them to start using passages and verses to help explain their faith and beliefs.

There are a number of lessons that can be learned from every Bible story. Fourth-graders should be able to share the lesson they learn from the story or passage. Asking good questions will become more and more important as students draw inferences. This is also a good time to start having students paraphrase and/or summarize the reading. They can retell a story or tell you what the reading was about in their own words.

In fourth grade, children should be able to describe characters, settings, and/or events in a story with detail and pick out words in the text that support their description. When reading the Bible they should be able to tell who is speaking or telling the story, what words or phrases tell you what somebody is feeling or thinking, etc. For example, when Elizabeth is told she would have a baby when she is 90 years old, she laughs. At this age, based on her reaction, children should be able to tell you what she is thinking or why she is laughing.

Tips for Teaching Fourth Grade

Some of the tips for third grade will also work with fourth grade. Based on what we know about fourth graders, here are some ideas:

- Fourth-graders should no longer be using a children's Bible. They need something more appropriate to their reading ability. Fewer pictures and more words. (Try Growing in Faith or Faith Alive.)
- Since fourth-graders have a tendency to be moody, be the lightness in the class. Enjoy their sense of humor, jokes, riddles, etc. Let go and laugh with them! Fourth grade is the perfect age for the silliness of Veggie Tales.
- Try to keep the direct instruction short and provide more opportunities for partner work, discussion, and projects.
- Craft your questions thoughtfully to engage their thinking. Focus less on who, what, when, and where, and more on how and why.
- Tap into their concern about right/wrong and ethics by asking what-would-you-do questions, put yourself in the Bible character's place questions, and ethical challenge questions based on the Bible story or passage.
- Use lame jokes or puns to cajole the kids into better behavior when necessary.
- Let them use dramatic reading when possible. This is a good time to bring the Bible alive by not only introducing Bible characters but also their personalities.
- Have lessons that focus on the Jewish culture. Sacrifices are difficult to understand without explanation.
- Give students the opportunity to do some Bible study with a partner. Provide worksheets for them to look words up and answer questions about what they're reading.
- Talk about moral decisions. People in the Bible were not perfect. The story of David and his choices is complex. He started off so well, what went wrong and how did it end for him?
- Don't tell them what unknown words mean. Let them use resources to discover meanings themselves.
- Use Bible maps so they get to know the country.
- Take the time to talk about how the Israelites lived. What is the significance of the well? How were women treated in a family? What's the story behind having 200 wives and concubines? Why was that okay?

- After reading the story, give each team the challenge of putting together a description of a character in it.
- Have student teams draw illustrations and retell the story to each other. Let other groups determine if they've forgotten critical elements.
- Fourth-graders enjoy drama. Let them put on skits to retell the story or let them be journalists and report the story.
- Be sure they leave class knowing that they have nothing to worry about because God is in control.

Knowledge Stage

CHAPTER 10

Fifth Grade

Fifth-graders are not slightly taller fourth-graders. Fifth grade is a time of change, or at least the beginning of change as children will begin moving into adolescence. They are social and can take on almost anything and have a good time doing it. They especially enjoy outside activities and group games.

Social and Emotional

Fifth-graders are generally happy and friendly. They usually look up to their teachers and parents and enjoy spending time with family and friends. They may be quick to anger, but are also quick to forgive; and are comfortable with both male and female friends. With the onset of puberty right around the corner, peer relationships take on greater meaning and they may believe friends over their parents.

Being cooperative and flexible, fifth-graders like group activities, collaborative or project-based learning, and team building activities. They also enjoy both competitive and non-competitive activities. While they do well working in small groups, they also enjoy working in larger groups and putting on class plays and participating in community service projects. They enjoy discussing social and world problems and feel they have something to share.

Fifth-graders are increasingly able to resolve conflicts among peers regarding issues of fairness as they have a greater understanding of complex issues and a more mature sense of right and wrong. Arguments may flare up and be resolved as quickly. They love to talk, discuss, and share what they know with classmates through drama, choral readings, and songs. They like to be noticed and want to be encouraged.

When children are younger they may try many different activities and it is in the fifth grade that they are deciding what they truly like and dislike.

They may choose to stop taking dance or choose baseball over soccer as this is the time when they will commit to studying music, dance, or a particular sport. It is also the time when they begin thinking about how they will parent and treat their own children in the future.

In the fifth grade children face a lot of peer pressure. Girls will primarily show friendship through note writing and gossip about other children while boys will show friendship with high-fives, shoving, and other physical expressions. Girls may experience a first crush which may or may not be acknowledged.

Cognitive

Fifth-graders are increasingly able to think abstractly, are extraordinarily good at memorizing, and easily absorb factual information. They enjoy logic and practicing their reasoning skills, though they may not always make sense. Along with this they enjoy rules and solving social, local, and world problems, though they may not quite understand their complexity.

Eleven-year-olds are beginning to see multiple sides of an issue and appreciate others' perspectives. They enjoy discussion, though they may need to be reminded or taught the rules of discussion. Along this line, fifth-graders realize that thoughts are private and that people are different from them. It's during this time that they see others as different from themselves in greater detail and may compare their skills to those of others.

Children in fifth grade can organize their thoughts and plan, though they may struggle with the difference between fact and opinion. It is at this age that they being to be able to predict the consequences of an action.

Social media is now becoming increasingly important, especially if students have cell phones and unmonitored internet access. They may be getting a lot of their information from social media and internet sites and much of it may be incorrect. It is a good time to start talking about valid sources and the challenge of determining true or false information. This will be a challenge for them.

Fifth-graders begin to understand how things are connected, which is an important milestone. They are able to understand the effects of political decisions and how one person in a group can affect the whole group. These decisions will have a greater impact on Christians in the future.

Fifth-graders are beginning the move further into abstract thought and many are involved in classes for Holy Communion. When it comes to abstract ideas, talking about them is easier than writing about them. They can always recite answers they've memorized to try to explain what they understand, but the mystery of what happens during the Lord's Supper is not only difficult for children to fully understand, but also for adults. The goal, however, is not that they understand the mystery, but that they understand the need for personal examination, repentance, and forgiveness that comes with the body and blood of Christ.

Behavior

Fifth-graders love to talk – all the time. Provide times for them to talk in class, but expect them to be quiet when you need them to be quiet. Everything is not up for discussion.

As they can now see things from other perspectives, fifth-graders are able to resolve friendship and fairness issues. Peer pressure is beginning to be a greater issue as they have a greater desire to feel like they are a part of a group. Watch to make sure there are no kids who are loners. If two cannot work together, make a group of three.

Children in fifth-grade will benefit from group meetings to address class problems and as they become more independent it helps to have them be a part of an agreed-upon behavior process. "We can't have that kind of behavior in this class, why not?" "How do you think that makes people feel?" Fifth-graders typically know all the rules, and have learned that it pays to be truthful, but as they grow they will test limits to find out which rules are negotiable and which are not. If every rule is negotiable then there are no rules. This is a good time to teach mediation and problem-solving so that everyone wins.

Children in fifth-grade are getting to the point where you can have a discussion with them about their behavior and why it needs to change, but don't do it in front of their peers. Have them step outside the room for a little chat. They respond well to positive adult recognition.

Bible Reading

In the fifth grade children should be able to quote accurately from the Bible when explaining what the text says and when making inferences. For example: What does God mean by "corrupt" in the time of Noah? What does that tell us about behavior today?

Fifth-graders should also be able to determine a theme of a Bible story from details in the text, including how people in a story respond to challenges. The story of David and Bathsheba is an obvious example of this. Don't accept only the obvious theme of sleeping with another man's wife. There are so many other places to take it.

Eleven-year-olds should also be able to accurately summarize the text. This does not have to be done in a written form. It can be presented as a skit, a poem, a song, etc. They can even write a children's story and illustrate it if there's time. It could also be as simple as, "Tell me what happened here."

Being able to compare and contrast two or more characters, settings, or events in a story is an important skill. We often forget that the characters or people in the Bible were real living human beings like us. We are also characters in God's story. How are we alike and different from those in the Bible? How is the event of Daniel in the lion's den similar and different from Shadrach, Meshach, and Abednego in the fiery furnace? Fifth-graders should be able to draw on specific details in the text to answer these questions and learn something about themselves in doing so.

There are numerous words and phrases in the Bible that are unfamiliar to children and adults. Some can be determined through context. Figurative language can be a challenge, but since fifth-graders are becoming more abstract they should be able to understand metaphors and similes like the "Spirit of God descending *like* a dove and coming to rest on Him." What characteristics does the Holy Spirit have then?

Interest in reading independently becomes stronger in the fifth grade so this would be a good time to have Bible reading challenges. Those students who read so many chapters or books can earn a Bible Reading Challenge certificate or you could create Bible reading punch cards. Be sure to create a list they can read that is interesting and not too much of a challenge. Reading Genesis and Exodus are far more interesting than Leviticus and Numbers, especially for kids.

Tips for Teaching Fifth Grade

Some of the tips for fourth grade will also work with fifth grade. Based on what we know about fifth-graders, here are some ideas:

- Fifth-graders need a Bible that is appropriate for their reading abilities. Fewer pictures and more words. (Try the Growing in Faith or Faith Alive.)
- Try to keep the direct instruction short and provide more opportunities for partner and group work, discussion, projects, and inquiry. Make sure projects require them to dig into the Bible and use the verses, passages, and stories to support the project.
- Since they like to talk, provide plenty of opportunity for partner chats about the Bible story or passage.
- When discussing in groups, be sure to have appropriately challenging questions to guide the discussion.
- Craft your questions thoughtfully to engage their thinking. Focus less on who, what, when, and where, and more on how and why.
- Tap into their growing ability to resolve conflicts by discussing how life choices and Bible concepts affect each other. Every choice we make can bring us closer to or take us away from Jesus.
- Talk about social media! Go through and save some memes and have the kids discuss how they affect each of them and society as a whole from a Christian world view.

- Tap into their concern about right/wrong and ethics by creating scenarios both from the Bible and society. Ask how they would respond to the issue.

- Every person in the Bible faces a problem or challenge to their faith. Look at the person or event they face and talk about what each person would do in that case. Some of the more challenging events are in the New Testament: What if you were in Peter's shoes and people confronted you about being one of Jesus' followers? What if you were the rich man and Jesus told you to get rid of everything? Get real about it.

- Now that they can see things from different perspectives, it's important for them to see that some things happen differently because of cultural differences. Talk about the similarities and differences. Use a chart or worksheet to help organize thoughts.

- Fifth-graders are entering into the life stage where their peers and fitting into a group will be extremely important. Talk about who they can go to when peer pressure gets to be too much.

- Let them use dramatic reading when possible. Continue to bring the Bible alive by not only introducing Bible characters but also their personalities. Read with inflection. Also have them do skits, choral reading, or songs.

- Give students the opportunity to do some Bible research with a partner. Provide worksheets for them to look words up and answer questions about what they're reading.

- Let kids work together to move more toward Bible Inquiry than study when it comes to reading and learning. What does this say? What do these words or phrases mean? What's going on in this story? Who are the characters? Use Bible Inquiry guide sheets.

- Talk about moral decisions. People in the Bible were not perfect. The story of David and his choices is complex. He started off so well, what went wrong and how did it end for him?

- Use Bible maps so they get to know the country.

- Take the time to talk about how the Israelites lived. What is the significance of the well? How were women treated in a family? What's the story behind wives and concubines? Why was that okay?

PART III

UNDERSTANDING STAGE
Grade 6 through Grade 8

The Understanding Stage is the middle school years; the confirmation years. It's at this age that kids begin to think more analytically. While still important to know, the facts become less important than why things happened. Students think more logically and notice when things don't make sense to them and they step deeper into Bible Inquiry. Why did God flood the earth? How does this affect me? Why were the people so evil? What does it mean to be righteous? Why does God need us to be holy? Couldn't God just make everything okay? The implications of the stories begin to have much deeper meaning and we want to encourage questions. Students seek to understand the Bible more fully in the Understanding Stage as it taps into how they feel or think about what they know about the Bible and the world. It's time to have discussions about the challenges of following God's Word and making it a part of their lives. It is time for them to come to an understanding of their faith and beliefs.

Now we have received not the spirit of the world, but the Spirit who is from God, that we might understand the things freely given us by God. 1 Corinthians 2:12 ESV

Understanding Stage

CHAPTER 11

Middle School

Middle schoolers are at the beginning of adolescence which is a busy time for minds and bodies. Aside from the first three years of life, there is no other time when the brain goes through so much change as during adolescence (Elmore, 2012). Early teens are preoccupied with physical and emotional changes as well as their social status while hormones are released throughout the body. Keep in mind that people grow and develop at different rates and that is true for puberty and adolescence.

Social and Emotional

The middle schooler's world view is broadening to include the world. In elementary school they rely primarily on what their parents tell them. In middle school they start seeing their world as a much larger place. They begin comparing how they were raised to what they see in the world on their journey to discover their personal identity, develop their self-concept, and build their self-esteem. It is the beginning of a time of wondering, searching, and seeking the truth of who they are and finding their purpose, which continues into adulthood. They are choosing their own friends and allowing those friends to influence their choices and share life experiences, and they may try on different identities and personalities. They don't always come to their parents with life questions anymore, but seek advice from friends instead. Middle schoolers:

- Are very self-absorbed, thinking nobody has ever been through what they are going through.
- May be impulsive and/or rude without realizing it.
- Make decisions based on emotions.
- Are looking for role models.

In middle school the need to have a social life and be a part of a group becomes very important. Kids are coming to Sunday school because it is expected by their parents (and may be a confirmation requirement), but they choose to attend primarily because they want to see their friends. Whether or not a student's friendship group attends church (either the same or a different church) has an effect on individual students' religious attendance and their perceptions of the importance of religion (Regnerus et al., 2004).

Discovering personal identity is a process of comparison. By comparing how they were raised and the beliefs they were raised into to that of their friends and society, kids begin the process of deciding who they want to be and what moral philosophy they want to live by. It is a challenging time because while they are pulling away from their parents and figuring out their place among their peers, parents worry. Comments made by important adults in the child's life, as well as their peers, can have a great positive or negative effect on their identity and feelings regarding how they see themselves (Langhoff, 2014). Low self-esteem develops if there is a discrepancy between a child's self-concept and what they think they *should* be (Harter as cited in APA, 2002) or who they think they are versus who they think they should be.

Most middle schoolers have unlimited cell phone and internet use, therefore, the media plays a prominent role in developing middle schoolers' identity. They are bombarded with messages of what the best life should be and few of those messages include God. There will be a lot of pressure to be like others and they may experiment with sex, drinking alcohol, smoking, and/or drugs. The strength of peer pressure and friend choice should not be taken lightly.

Cognitive

In middle school, the brain is a bit past the middle of its development. Look at the picture below of the brain to see where that falls.

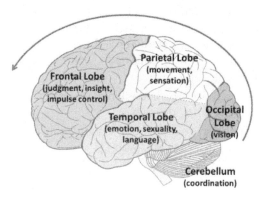

76

In *The Teenage Brain*, Frances Jensen (2015) reminds us that the temporal lobe, which contains emotion, sexuality, and language, is developed before the frontal lobe which contains impulse control, judgment, and insight. So, when middle school rolls around the frontal lobe is the least mature and connected part of the brain (Jensen, 2015). Middle schoolers are beginning their journey into independence without fully developed impulse control, risk assessment, and judgment. Their reason, logic, and ability to predict the future is less developed than their emotional push to react to things. At the same time, life is much less black and white than it used to be and they are investigating its many gray areas.

Middle school students:

- Can increasingly think of the world from different perspectives.
- Love to argue and debate, but may argue for the sake of arguing as their reasoning skills may not be quite on point. Consider it practice.
- Have a limited world view with regard to experience and understanding.
- Forget what they're asked to do.
- Don't often consider the consequences of their actions.
- Rarely think in terms of the future, though they have the ability to do so.
- Begin to want more independence without responsibility.
- Need to make some choices for themselves. Give reasonable choices.
- Still enjoy hands-on activities but are developing abstract abilities.

During early adolescence, middle schoolers begin seeing that *yes* and *no* are not the only answers to most of life's questions. They begin to see that their behavior has consequences beyond parental punishment. They also enjoy testing their reasoning ability and may argue for the sake of arguing. You may find that when you have discussion their reasoning may not be sound (Vawter, 2010 and APA, 2002).

From this time forward, in Christian education, it is important to allow kids to develop their thoughts and opinions, challenging them with *why* they believe what they do. While our instinct and habit is to tell them what to believe, this is the time to be sure we do not do that. This is the time to make sure we ask questions to help them come to their beliefs with the help of the Holy Spirit, and allow them to ask any questions they might have. Do not ignore their questions.

Physical

Middle schoolers are experiencing major body changes as their bodies prepare for sexual activity and reproduction. In general, many of those changes are (*No Child Left Behind*, 2005):

- Their sex organs are coming alive.
- There may be rapid skeletal growth that could cause growing pains.
- They are overly aware of their own body changes.
- They are also very aware of how their friends' bodies are changing.
- The physical changes distract from other pursuits.
- They start comparing their bodies to those of their same sex friends.
- They start noticing the changes in the opposite sex.
- They begin feeling physical attraction to the opposite sex.
- They begin to have body odor.
- They begin to have acne.
- They have hair growing in places they don't want to mention.
- Hormones, hormones, hormones!

Society's view of sex as a recreational activity starts being far more noticeable for children in middle school, especially as sexual feelings and attraction becomes real and exciting. These feelings along with the Biblical view and societal view of sex can also be very confusing.

Girls enter puberty about 18 months earlier than do boys. This is why you may hear girls talking about boys and boys talking about sports.

Behavior

Middle schoolers are very self-absorbed. You may often hear the phrase, "You just don't get it!" While every one of us has been there, they think nobody has ever been through what they are going through. Be aware that middle schoolers make decisions based on their emotions, not assessing consequences and risks.

Friends are extremely important at this time, but kids this age can be mean and defensive about mistakes. Girls typically form cliques and boys have small groups of friends. Feeling excluded is the worst thing that can happen at this age. Be aware of students being left out and make sure everyone in the class feels like a part of the group. If you do partner work, choose the partners so that friends don't choose friends and nobody is singled out as not being chosen. If you need to address an issue, pull them aside, speak to them in the hallway, and let them know that their behavior is not working for you, which means it's not working for them.

Kids in middle school may be impulsive and/or rude without realizing it to both peers and adults. Remind them of what rude is without making a huge issue of it. They like to challenge rules too and may try to debate or argue their way around them. Stand your ground.

For middle school and high school I typically have 3 major rules:

> **Respect for the Learning Environment**—This may include being on time, not disrupting class, not using electronic devices, or not eating food without permission.
>
> **Respect for Property**—This may include no gum, not sitting on or writing on tables, and taking care of books.
>
> **Respect for Each Other**—This may include speaking to and treating each other well, not borrowing without asking, keeping your hands to yourself, and using appropriate language.

Zero Tolerance

Disrespect seems to run rampant among adolescents today. They seem to believe that they are allowed to speak their mind whenever they want. There should be zero tolerance for disrespect. It doesn't help that when they are verbally disrespectful they often get positive feedback from other students. Some parents allow their children to disrespect them in the home without consequence. Students who are mean or disrespectful to the teacher or other students should be expected to make it right. First, give the look of disappointment and see if they apologize right away. If not, ask them out into the hallway and then ask them why they are out there. Don't take much time away from class. If they don't know why they're out there, have them stay there and think about it a bit. Tell them you'll be back to see if they've figured it out in a few minutes. When they realize they've been disrespectful or mean, ask them what they can do to make it right.

Try to handle discipline issues without involving the parents. It sends a message that you can't handle the class and middle schoolers know that. If something happens that you think parents should know about, walk the student to the parent and say, "Hopefully things will go better for you next week." The next question from the parent should be directed to the student: "What happened?"

Tips for Teaching Middle School

Sunday school or Sunday Bible Inquiry meets once a week. In many churches this is the only time available to impact students with Biblical truth even while Biblical literacy is at an all-time low for Christians of all ages. In order to address this problem most people who write curriculum for middle school try to make it fun and/or entertaining, and interactive in all the wrong ways. What students truly want is to find the truth and to learn it in a way that's interesting and meaningful. What does that look like?

- Start talking about why people believe what they do and why they do what they do. Don't stop asking *why*.

- Try some moral or ethical dilemmas. Every person in the Bible had a choice to make. What are the pros and cons? What if Noah didn't build the ark? What if Noah let other people on the ark? What would happen if…?

- When discussing the Bible, try looking at stories or beliefs from different perspectives and allow them to struggle with them and come up with their own conclusions… with your guidance. Why don't some churches baptize babies?

- As they are beginning to wonder about their own moral standards, provide opportunities for them to discuss ethics and Christian teachings. Why does God have things we shouldn't do?

- Allow them to struggle with concepts and find their way to their own conclusions by giving them things to think about… pieces of puzzles they can put together logically. This may require looking at a bigger picture.

- They can and should cite several pieces of contextual evidence to support analysis of what the text says. It's not because it makes sense to you, it's because it makes sense to God and He knows more than you.

- Determine a central idea of a text (there may be many in Bible accounts). Have them write it down and put them in a jar. Nobody wants to think they're wrong because they came up with something different. Put them all on the wall/board and discuss how each applies.

- Determine the meaning of words and phrases used in the text. Use a concordance or Bible dictionary as much as possible.

- Compare a written story to what is portrayed in the media. How much of what is seen in the media is true?

- Use a Bible timeline so students see where the Bible fits in historically.

- Have students create a detailed plot outline of complicated stories like Joseph or Moses. Add sections where God acted and the result of that action.

- Put each account studied into the bigger picture of God's relationship with his people.

- Be sure to bring up the differences in culture during Bible eras and compare them to today's culture.

- FACILITATE discussion – lead them to a conclusion without telling them what it is. Questions, questions, questions.

- Give them things to think about but don't tell them what to think about it.
- Since middle schoolers have difficulty determining consequences, make sure that's a part of discussion.
- Try making them support the opposite side of the argument or split them into two sides and make them convince the other that they are right.
- Start talking about the beauty of sex and intimacy now in a Biblical context. Don't merely tell them to say *no*! Tell them why God tells us not to have sex outside of marriage. How will that affect them later?
- They enjoy interacting with each other more than the teacher, so unless the class is very small, let them.
- Make them USE THE BIBLE.
- Make them think about everything!!

CHAPTER 12

Middle School Bible Inquiry

The middle school years are the perfect time to start teaching Bible Inquiry instead of having Bible study. Bible study is about sitting in a group, listening and answering a few questions, and maybe doing a word search puzzle. Bible Inquiry is about probing for the truth, seeking to learn through queries or questions, investigating, discussing. To participate in Bible Inquiry is not to sit and listen. It's to dig and discover! This requires the ability to craft questions in a way that requires more than obvious answers and includes the expectation that kids will discuss, debate, and grow. Teenagers, more than deep theological research, want to know how the Bible is connected to them. What truth does it hold for them and why? What does Bible Inquiry look like at the middle school level? First we'll address what it doesn't look like.

When looking at a curriculum or lessons for your middle school Bible studies:

1) Remind yourself of where your students are developmentally, then...
2) Look at the goal, key point, or central truth and keep it in mind as you peruse the lesson.
3) Be sure the Bible reading connects to the goal, key point, or central truth.
4) Look at the questions to see if they are too obvious, too literal, redundant, or won't challenge the students. (I.e. the answer is "Jesus died for our sins.")
5) Check to make sure the questions lead the students to the goal.
6) Be sure the lesson doesn't tell students what to think or that the key point in the reading is so vague that they will not find it without help.

7) Check for any unnecessary *non-educational* activities like games, word games or puzzles, crafts, or activities that are below grade level and are busy-work.

Below is a lesson called Rebecca Serves at the Well from a Growing in Christ Summer curriculum (Schilf, 2012). The lessons in this curriculum have a key point or goal of the lesson, Law/Gospel Points, and further connections. There is also a nice commentary on the scripture to help inform the teacher.

Typical Published Lesson

On the left below is the scripture and on the right are the questions from the lesson and a bit of commentary.

Rebecca Serves at the Well	Genesis 24:10-28 ESV
[10]Then the servant took ten of his master's camels and departed, taking all sorts of choice gifts from his master; and he arose and went to Mesopotamia to the city of Nahor. [11]And he made the camels kneel down outside the city by the well of water at the time of evening, the time when women go out to draw water. [12]And he said, "O Lord, God of my master Abraham, please grant me success today and show steadfast love to my master Abraham. [13]Behold, I am standing by the spring of water, and the daughters of the men of the city are coming out to draw water. [14]Let the young woman to whom I shall say, 'Please let down your jar that I may drink,' and who shall say, 'Drink, and I will water your camels'—let her be the one whom you have appointed for your servant Isaac. By this I shall know that you have shown steadfast love to my master." [15]Before he had finished speaking, behold, Rebekah, who was born to Bethuel the son of Milcah, the wife of Nahor, Abraham's brother, came out with her water jar on her shoulder.	**As you read, think about how God allowed Rebekah, and Abraham's servant to serve and to live their vocations.** (Connecting this passage to vocation seems like a stretch for middle schoolers.) **How did the servant love and serve his master, Abraham? How do we know that he trusted the Lord?** (He did what he was asked to do. He trusted God because he prayed.) **In what ways did the servant serve his master, Abraham?** (He did what he was asked to do.) (These 2 questions are essentially the same and are very obvious.)
[16]The young woman was very attractive in appearance, a maiden whom no man had known. She went down to the spring and filled her jar and came up. [17]Then the servant ran to meet her and said, "Please give me a little water to drink from your	**How did Rebekah love and serve Abraham's servant?** (She freely gave water. This question is a partner to the others and is also very obvious.) **Why did Rebekah water the servant's**

84

jar." [18]She said, "Drink, my lord." And she quickly let down her jar upon her hand and gave him a drink. [19]When she had finished giving him a drink, she said, "I will draw water for your camels also, until they have finished drinking." [20]So she quickly emptied her jar into the trough and ran again to the well to draw water, and she drew for all his camels. [21]The man gazed at her in silence to learn whether the Lord had prospered his journey or not.	camels? (There could be many answers to this. One might be that she was being hospitable as was the custom. Another might be because she was being nice; and another could be an attempt to connect the reading to the fourth petition of the Lord's Prayer, "give us this day our daily bread." The reading does not indicate.)
[22]When the camels had finished drinking, the man took a gold (*nose) ring weighing a half shekel, and two bracelets for her arms weighing ten gold shekels, [23]and said, "Please tell me whose daughter you are. Is there room in your father's house for us to spend the night?" [24]She said to him, "I am the daughter of Bethuel the son of Milcah, whom she bore to Nahor." [25]She added, "We have plenty of both straw and fodder, and room to spend the night." [26]The man bowed his head and worshiped the Lord [27]and said, "Blessed be the Lord, the God of my master Abraham, who has not forsaken his steadfast love and his faithfulness toward my master. As for me, the Lord has led me in the way to the house of my master's kinsmen." [28]Then the young woman ran and told her mother's household about these things.	**How did God work through the humans in the Bible story to show His love?** (The servant prayed that God show him the chosen woman by having her water the camels and God moved Rebekah to water the camels.)
Application Question(s)	**When you are asked to do something difficult, how do you respond?** (various answers) **Who has done something very difficult for you?** (Jesus.)
Application Statements	**We may want to be recognized for our work, but because Jesus died for us we are free to serve others even if it's inconvenient. Jesus has done the real work for us. Because of Him, we have salvation.**

Please note the obvious questions that do not challenge. Also, the connections are tenuous at best. The goal of Bible Inquiry is to design the lesson so that students look more closely at the passage and answer questions that challenge them at their developmental level and drive them to make connections themselves.

There is more to the lesson above such as a verse to remember and a short game so students can say it three or four times, a vocation word search puzzle, and a game about guessing vocations (waiter, electrician, doctor, etc.). There is also an attempt at a connection to the fourth petition, "Give us this day our daily bread," and since Rebekah got a bracelet from Abraham's servant, there is a craft of an edible bracelet and a suggestion of a fruit snack. Nothing in this lesson is at the middle school developmental level (except serving food) and it is quite a stretch to connect this reading to vocation and the fourth petition of the Lord's Prayer. How would Bible Inquiry work?

Bible Inquiry Lesson

Recall that Bible Inquiry is about questions, investigation, and discussion, though middle schoolers are not great discussers yet. The over-arching story of the Old Testament is how we get from Adam and Eve to Jesus, and why. Within that story is the story of God's relationship with his chosen people; within that story are stories of how He uses them to reach his goal of saving them and bringing them back into his presence. It is the playing out of Genesis 3:15 ("I will put enmity between you and the woman, and between your offspring and her offspring; he shall bruise your head, and you shall bruise his heel.")

Culture, politics, and geography (climate and weather) can play a huge part in understanding some parts of the Bible. They tell why people travel certain routes, why they make the choices they make, why groups don't marry other groups, and many other things. In the lesson below an understanding of how spouses were chosen, the placement of the well in a community, and the significance of hospitality to strangers are important to understanding this passage. They also help develop the attitude of inquiry in Bible Inquiry.

Bible Inquiry Lesson	
God Gives Isaac a Wife	Genesis 24:2-4, 10-28 ESV
There are a few themes we will look at with this lesson. 1. Finding a spouse 2. Hospitality 3. Prayer 4. Trusting God	
Read the passage as a large group, then put students in groups of 2 or 3 to answer the questions.	
²And Abraham said to his servant, the oldest of his household, who had charge of all that he had, "Put your hand under my thigh, ³that I may make you swear by	Put 2 categories on the board or wall: THEN -- NOW **With highlighters, have students read the passage again and highlight anything that**

the LORD, the God of heaven and God of the earth, that you will not take a wife for my son from the daughters of the Canaanites, among whom I dwell, ⁴but will go to my country and to my kindred, and take a wife for my son Isaac." ¹⁰Then the servant took ten of his master's camels and departed, taking all sorts of choice gifts from his master; and he arose and went to Mesopotamia to the city of Nahor. ¹¹And he made the camels kneel down outside the city by the well of water at the time of evening, the time when women go out to draw water. ¹²And he said, "O Lord, God of my master Abraham, please grant me success today and show steadfast love to my master Abraham. ¹³Behold, I am standing by the spring of water, and the daughters of the men of the city are coming out to draw water. ¹⁴Let the young woman to whom I shall say, 'Please let down your jar that I may drink,' and who shall say, 'Drink, and I will water your camels'—let her be the one whom you have appointed for your servant Isaac. By this I shall know that you have shown steadfast love to my master."

¹⁵Before he had finished speaking, behold, Rebekah, who was born to Bethuel the son of Milcah, the wife of Nahor, Abraham's brother, came out with her water jar on her shoulder. ¹⁶The young woman was very attractive in appearance, a maiden whom no man had known. She went down to the spring and filled her jar and came up. ¹⁷Then the servant ran to meet her and said, "Please give me a little water to drink from your jar." ¹⁸She said, "Drink, my lord." And she quickly let down her jar upon her hand and gave him a drink. ¹⁹When she had finished giving him a drink, she said, "I will draw water for your camels also, until they have finished

they think is a cultural difference.

What seems odd to you in this passage? (Answers vary. Somebody is picking out somebody else's spouse, the servant puts a nose ring on her and takes her, the oath of putting his hand under Abraham's thigh, he's never met her, but asks if he can stay at her father's house, etc. Have students write their observations about cultural differences on large sticky notes so they can be categorized.) Look at them. **What are some pros and cons of how these things were done then?**

It turns out it's a pretty modern concept for people to choose their own spouse. Arranged marriages still take place in some countries. **Read the cultural information as a large group.**

Why did Abraham send his servant away to find a wife for Isaac and not pick someone local? Canaanites were outside the covenant between God and Abraham. **What does this concern tell us about marriage?** Who you choose is a BIG deal.

———————————————

Imagine you're outside watering the garden and a stranger comes up and asks for a drink from your hose. What would you do? He mentions that he's headed somewhere. What are your instincts? (Allow students to respond, writing answers on the board.) **If they need prompting ask, "Do you:**
   Offer him the hose?
   Have a friendly conversation?
   Invite him in for a drink?
   Offer him some food?
What would your parents say if you did these things?"

Read Genesis 18:2-8, 19:1-3, Exodus 23:9. Discuss in groups.

drinking." [20]So she quickly emptied her jar into the trough and ran again to the well to draw water, and she drew for all his camels. [21]The man gazed at her in silence to learn whether the Lord had prospered his journey or not.

[22]When the camels had finished drinking, the man took a gold (*nose) ring weighing a half shekel, and two bracelets for her arms weighing ten gold shekels, [23]and said, "Please tell me whose daughter you are. Is there room in your father's house for us to spend the night?" [24]She said to him, "I am the daughter of Bethuel the son of Milcah, whom she bore to Nahor." [25]She added, "We have plenty of both straw and fodder, and room to spend the night." [26]The man bowed his head and worshiped the Lord [27]and said, "Blessed be the Lord, the God of my master Abraham, who has not forsaken his steadfast love and his faithfulness toward my master. As for me, the Lord has led me in the way to the house of my master's kinsmen." [28]Then the young woman ran and told her mother's household about these things.

*This is more likely a nose-ring as they were not unusual and a present of a single earring for two ears would be strange (Freeman, 1972).

What is hospitality? (The friendly and generous reception and entertainment of guests, visitors, or strangers.)

What is a sojourner? (A short-term visitor.)

Why did Rebekah give water to Abraham's servant and camels? (She was showing them typical and expected hospitality.)

Look at the two categories on the board. After reading about the culture of the time, students should have a conversation about how our culture now is different from then in those areas. Think of hospitality, neighbors, traveling, etc. Add our cultural differences next to the other sticky notes.

What do you think of how Isaac was getting his wife? What are the pros and cons of that practice? What are the pros and cons of their idea of hospitality and how they treat travelers versus ours? Are our ways much better or worse than theirs? What might we learn from them?

The servant had a tough job. Who knew how it would turn out? **When you have something challenging to do, how do you face it? Where do you get your courage? When it goes well, how do you respond?**

Look back at the reading one more time and find God in it. How did the servant face his challenge and how did he respond when it was successful? What can you do in your life to acknowledge God in how you face your challenges?

Practice looking to God in everyday problems. *Dear Solomon* exercise. Pass one "letter" to each group. Below are examples. Feel free to write your own.

In your groups, write a response to each letter, keeping in mind how the servant handled his problem.

	Dear Solomon: I have to tell my mom that I'm failing math before my teacher does. Any advice?
	Dear Solomon: All my friends have boyfriends and I don't. I'm not even sure if I want one. Is there something wrong with me? Help!
	Dear Solomon: I don't have a lot of friends at school and wish I had a best friend. What can I do?
	We need to remind each other to trust God, talk to Him, and praise Him for His great, enduring, and everlasting love.

Here is what a possible handout might contain.

Shortened version of student handout.	
Read Genesis 24:2-4, 10-28. Highlight anything you think is a cultural difference from today. What seems odd to you in this passage? Write them on sticky notes and put them in the THEN category on the board. With your group, list some pros and cons of doing things the way they did then?	
Read the verses below and write down what they say about hospitality and a sojourner.	
Genesis 18:2-8	
Genesis 9:1-3	
Exodus 23:9	
What is hospitality and how are they to treat sojourners? How is their idea of hospitality different from ours? What is a sojourner? Was Rebecca going above and beyond in showing them hospitality?	
What do you think of how Isaac was getting his wife? What are the pros and cons of that practice? What are the pros and cons of their idea of hospitality and how they treat travelers versus ours? What might we learn from them?	
Look back at the reading (Genesis 24:2-4, 10-28) again and find God in it. List where and how God shows up. How did the servant face his challenge and how did he respond when he was successful? What can you do in your life to acknowledge God in how you face your challenges?	

Have basic cultural information available.

Culture in the Time of Isaac

During Isaac's time, it was typical for the groom not to choose his bride. The parents (or both fathers) would negotiate a marriage contract as a matter of business and the bride and groom were expected to accept the decision. It was very important for Abraham that his son have a wife within the covenant and not a Canaanite.

In the east, water was scarce and wells were usually built outside the city because of their constant use, noise, and dust. It was the "work" of women to fill the water jugs in the morning and evening and they all usually went at the same time. Abraham's servant stopped at the well because he knew the women would be coming to get water.

Hospitality was an important virtue and it focused on the travelers because they were not a part of the community and were dependent on strangers for food and lodging. Hospitality was receiving a traveler into your home for food, lodging and/or protection, allowing them to harvest the corners of your field, providing them clothing, feeding the poor, and accepting them into your worship service or religious celebrations. The Israelites were expected to show hospitality as an act of righteous behavior. It was expected that people would take care of travelers; invite them in for food, give them a place to sleep, and take care of their animals whenever possible. Jewelry was a present a rich man gave to a possible wife to prove he had wealth and to bind the marriage contract.

The Bible Inquiry lesson has students interact with scripture much more than the other lesson. While in groups, students work together to analyze the Word. It also provides them thoughtful application questions and more to think about from a real-life standpoint.

Part IV

REASON STAGE
Grade 9 through Grade 12

The Reason Stage is for high school and college aged students. It builds on the first three stages, using knowledge and understanding to really dig deep into Bible Inquiry and question. It tries to see how what they know applies directly to their lives. In high school students are searching for the truth of life, which is directly related to Scripture. A lot is going on in their bodies and lives at this time as they begin to become independent. They no longer want to be told what to do, think, or believe. They want to believe it on their own. They are developing reason and judgment and deciding what is true or false. The world and a lot of untruth are at their feet, or more accurately, their fingertips. At this stage allowing them to ask, and answering their questions becomes very important. How do we do that? How do we ask questions that will really get them to think? How do we challenge their faith so that they become comfortable and confident in it? It's important for them to make God's Word a part of their lives as they continue the journey of discovering their place in the world, embracing their faith and beliefs, and embracing who they want to become.

"...always being prepared to make a defense to anyone who asks you for a reason for the hope that is in you; yet do it with gentleness and respect,..." 1 Peter 3:15 ESV

Reason Stage

CHAPTER 13

High School

Teenagers are searching. They are in a very pivotal stage of life where they are running toward independence, but aren't quite ready for it. Middle school is the time when children begin their search for identity and where they fit in the world. In high school the search broadens and deepens. Unfortunately, in the church they are confirmed before the journey ends.

Teenage Brain and Hormones*

Frances Jensen, in The Teenage Brain (2015), describes the brain of a teenager as "like a brand-new Ferrari. It's primed and pumped, but hasn't been road tested yet." In the teenage years hormones are released and the brain has to learn how to deal with them. It is a lengthy process and high schoolers are in the middle of it. Both estrogen and progesterone rise and fall with girls' menstrual cycles. Those two hormones are linked to chemicals in the brain that control mood, which explains how a teenage girl can switch from being happy and laughing to crying and depressed as if a switch was flipped. Testosterone, which controls the fight or flight response, floods through boys affecting aggression or fear.

Estrogen, progesterone, and testosterone are also the sex hormones and they become active in the emotional center of the brain during the teen years. Emotionally, teens are unpredictable and they often look for emotionally charged experiences. They like emotional music, movies, and books; they may experiment with extreme amusement park rides, blowing things up, driving fast, and fire. Teens are challenged by a "jacked-up stimulus-seeking brain not yet fully capable of making mature decisions (Jensen, F., 2015)." It's important to know that it's not that teenagers have higher hormone levels than young adults, but their brains have to adjust to them so they react to them in unexpected ways. Jensen (2015) also says that "adolescent boys shave and teenage girls can get pregnant, but neurologically neither has a brain ready for adulthood."

Another way a teenage brain responds differently than an adult brain is with regard to stress. Teenagers seem to have more anxiety and panic disorders during puberty than at other times. In adults "the hormone THP is released to help regulate anxiety, but in teens it is shown to have the reverse effect, raising anxiety instead of reducing it," explains Jensen (2015). Stress can cause children to have trouble with grades, changes in behavior, sleep disturbances, headaches, stomach aches, or colds, avoid social situations or begin nervous habits like biting their nails.

Another challenge of the teenage brain is insight. Teenagers still struggle with the ability to look outside themselves as it takes place in the frontal and pre-frontal lobes, which takes time to develop. When it comes to the teenage brain, almost anything can happen. "Teenagers may look like adults, they may even think like adults in many ways, and their ability to learn is staggering, but knowing what teenagers are unable to do – what their cognitive, emotional, behavioral limitations are – is critically important."

*Jensen, Frances (2015). The Teenage Brain.

Teenage Brain and Dopamine

In Psychology Today, Weinschenk (2012) explains that dopamine, which was thought to cause pleasure, actually causes you to "want, desire, seek out, and search." It's dopamine that makes you curious and encourages you to look for information. Basically, it's the difference between wanting something and liking something. The dopamine system makes you want it and the opioid system makes you like it. Weinschenk (2012) says, "If your seeking isn't turned off at least for a little while, then you start to run in an endless loop. The dopamine system is stronger than the opioid system. You tend to seek more than you are satisfied."

On the internet or when texting, we often get instant or near-instant responses which can start the dopamine loop. You start seeking and then get a reward and start seeking more, but at some point your seeking overtakes your reward and it becomes harder and harder to stop because the dopamine system doesn't have the ability to be satisfied (Weinschenk, 2012). The level of dopamine in the teenage brain causes them to be more easily addicted (Jensen, 2015).

Unpredictability also stimulates the dopamine system as we never know when an email, text, or tweet will show up or who they will be from so having notification sounds enhance the addictive effect (Weinschenk, 2012). It's similar to when Pavlov did his study with dogs and soon when they heard a bell ring simply the idea that food was coming would cause them to salivate. Those noises set off the dopamine system as do short messages leaving you in anticipation of more information.

The problem with all of this is that the constant stimulation through notifications can be exhausting and the constant switching of attention makes it hard to truly focus. It is not multi-tasking. It is constantly switching from one thing to another and it makes getting things done and the ability to focus very difficult. When teenagers study with music, the internet, and their phones constantly vying for their attention they switch focus so often that they end up in a dopamine loop.

Physical

With the invasion of hormones, the bodies of adolescents go through a lot of change both inside and out as they prepare for the ability to reproduce. Physically girls develop earlier than boys. In early adolescence girls may seem more interested in boys than boys are in girls because of this. Along with growing body hair, girls' bodies develop curves as their breasts grow and their hips begin to widen. They typically have a growth spurt between about 10-18 years old. Boys also grow body hair, their testes enlarge and their voices deepen; their growth spurt is from about 12 to 22 years. The timing of puberty is not the same for every boy or girl and they notice. They may feel self-conscious if they perceive themselves developing earlier or later than their peers. Teenagers find themselves wanting to be unique as they try to fit in.

It is normal for teens to feel self-conscious and feel anxiety about their changing bodies and their appearance, however, it is also important to pay attention and address any difficulties they may have in dealing with these changes. Look for:

- Withdrawal or fear of body changes in early adolescence.
- An obsessive concern about their appearance.
- Excessive dieting or exercising.
- Depression connected to their bodies.
- Avoidance of social activities.

A small number of teens can have body dysmorphic disorder that goes beyond basic anxiety. Both boys and girls can have serious eating or body distortion disorders. These disorders are not a phase, can be very dangerous, and need professional help to conquer as they are a persistent delusion. The most prevalent for teens are (Mayo Clinic):

- **Anorexia Nervosa** – extreme weight loss and fear of weight gain. Warning signs might be dramatic weight loss, preoccupation with weight, food, calories, fat grams or dieting, excessive or obsessive exercise, and frequent comments about being overweight in spite of weight loss.
- **Bulimia Nervosa** – eating large amounts of food only to vomit or use laxatives to remove it. Warning signs might be evidence of

binge-eating or purging, a preoccupation with food, excessive or obsessive exercise, or any ritual behaviors that accompany binging and purging, especially around mealtime.

- **Body Dysmorphic Disorder** – an intense preoccupation or obsession with appearance or body image, usually focused on one area of the body. The perceived flaw and constant checking of it can cause distress and interruption of daily life. Areas of concern for teens are: face (nose, complexion, acne and other blemishes), muscle size and tone (the idea that your body is not lean and muscular enough). Warning signs are being preoccupied with flaws only the teen sees as something that makes them ugly; spending hours trying to "fix" the perceived problem through styling, grooming, and make-up or asking for surgery to correct the problem; working out and/or lifting weights to the point where it becomes a primary activity over school, social life, and family life. Muscle dysmorphia can lead to steroid use.

Teens that have a preoccupation with parts of their bodies through puberty usually grow out of them or things have a tendency to normalize for them as they age. If they don't it's important to know that body dysmorphic disorders, which vary and typically start in the early teen years, usually don't get better on their own (Mayo Clinic). Left on their own they can cause anxiety, severe depression, and thoughts of suicide. It is important to pay attention and seek professional help as needed.

Social and Emotional

By nature teenagers are very self-absorbed. They don't think about you as much as you may think they do. Their thoughts are on themselves first, their friends second, and other teens third. Adults fall somewhere after that.

As noted above, the physical development of teens has an effect on them both socially and emotionally. With the changes in their bodies and increase in sexual desires, teens are strongly attuned to any sex talk or innuendo. More girls than boys begin to develop emotional stress over not looking the way the think they should look compared to their friends. This is the time to constantly make casual comments about how God made everyone unique intentionally.

During the teen years the sense of identity develops more fully and becomes more cohesive. They become reflective of experiences and relationships. Friends and experiences have a lot to do with the identity building process. Teenagers will show increased interest in opposite-sex relationships, both friend and romantic, but friends of their same sex take priority and close friendships become more important. They will strongly identify with their peers and their need to be a part of a group becomes extremely important. It is natural and normal for teenagers to distance themselves from their parents as their independence increases.

Teenagers also have developed more with regard to understanding things from different perspectives and concern for others, and evidence of their conscience playing a bigger part in choices and relationships. They question moral rights and privileges more as their moral reasoning increases and may become involved in or outspoken regarding social, cultural, and family issues.

Cognitive

The teenage years are the perfect time for learning as teenagers learn faster than at any other time (Jensen, 2015). "Memories are easier to make and last longer when acquired in teen years compared with adult years" and "there is solid data to show that your IQ can change during your teenage years, more than anyone had ever expected," (Jensen, 2015). However, "just because their brains are learning at peak efficiency, doesn't change the fact that much else is inefficient such as: attention, self-discipline, task completion and emotions" (Jensen, 2015).

In the teenage years abstract thinking becomes fully developed and their intellectual interests expand and gain importance. They are able to compromise, make applications to their own lives, reflect on the choices of others, and think about the future. Their interests, however, tend to focus on the present and near-future.

In short, three main areas of cognitive development in the teenage years are centered around strengthening:

- **Reasoning skills** – thinking about multiple possibilities, thinking about hypotheticals, following a logical thought process.
- **Abstract thinking skills** – thinking about things that can't be seen, heard, or touched such as faith, love, trust, beliefs and spirituality.
- **Thinking about thinking** (meta-cognition) – thinking about how they feel and what they are thinking as well as what others perceive about them.

Though it may appear so, cognitive ability in teenagers is not at the adult level yet. They can think ideas through, but their logic can be faulty. In her book, *The Teenage Brain* (2015), Frances Jensen tells the story of a boy who was stopped by the police for driving 113 mph and was given a speeding ticket. Though he admitted he was driving far faster than the speed limit, he was furious because the ticket was for *reckless driving* and he said he was not reckless. He had planned the whole thing out choosing both the road and time of day to drive 113 mph carefully. What he couldn't see was all the possible things that could have gone terribly wrong causing reckless thinking leading to reckless driving.

Music

Whether it's rock, country, or any other genre, music plays a large and important role in the life of a teenager. They listen primarily for three reasons: to help create a social image, satisfy emotional needs, and enjoyment (North et al., as cited in Miranda, 2013).

Adolescents seem to have a stronger connection to music than at any other time of life, say Roberts and collaborators (as cited in Miranda, 2013). Research shows that there is a reason for this. As already noted, the teen years are fraught with anxiety. A lot is happening at this time biologically, physical, socially, and emotionally. Their brains are on emotional overload. Their bodies are exploding with hormones making sex a prevalent player in their lives in a society that tells them that it is the answer to all happiness. They're seeing the world as a very huge and complex place with huge and complex problems and realize that they live in a society that is far from good. They are questioning morality as they see (but may not understand why) bad things happen to good people and that sometimes the people in charge are not good people. They wonder why God doesn't fix all it. They are also discovering that their parents are human and make mistakes; sometimes big ones.

Music is the soundtrack to life during the teenage years as adolescents listen to music up to three hours a day (Roberts et al., as cited in Miranda, 2013). It fills emotional needs and is often used to distract them from negative emotions such as loneliness, sadness, anger, or frustration; it helps them find solace and validation (Schwartz & Fouts, as cited in Miranda, 2013). Teenagers use music to help cope with stress they may feel, but can't put their finger on and problems they aren't sure how to solve. Research shows that youth use music to manage and avoid their emotions when depressed (Miranda and Claes, as cited in Miranda, 2013).

Music has a powerful influence on mood. The music listened to can affect mood positively or negatively. Anderson, Carnagey, and Eubanks (as cited in Miranda, 2013) found that anti-social songs seem to influence antisocial thoughts and feelings. It was determined by Selfhout, Delsing, ter Bogt, & Meeus (as cited in Miranda, 2013), that during adolescence listening to music genres that express controversial or negative themes, such as heavy metal, hip-hop, and rap, can predict acting on problem behaviors. Basically, repeated exposure to negative or aggressive songs can lead to aggressive behavior in *some* vulnerable teens.

Unfortunately, research by Martino and collaborators (as cited in Miranda, 2013) shows that "adolescents' exposure to music with degrading sexual lyrics predicted early sexual activities and intercourse.".

It should also be noted that while some songs may have a negative impact on depression symptoms, the favorite songs of teens can have a positive impact on or act as a protective factor against internalizing depression symptoms (Miranda, 2013). Listening to songs with positive lyrics or messages that convey resilience, coping, self-determination, faith, and trust in God can work against feelings of depression. Introducing teenage students to different styles of Christian music may encourage them to use Biblical or Christian messages to help them cope with the stresses of life moving toward independence amid the hormonal storm.

Social Media

Teenagers live very public lives due to their constant use of social media. They post thousands of photos of themselves and personal information, not realizing that there could be serious consequences. At no time in history have teenagers had the ability to make themselves so visible to unknown, possibly dangerous people and this ability has risks (Herring & Kapidzic, 2015).

By the time children become teenagers, their screen time rises to about 7.5 hours a day with even more time spent doing what is called media multitasking for a total daily screen time of about 11 hours (Herring & Kapidzic, 2015). Media multitasking is using more than one media at a time. Often, while studying, teenagers will be listening to music and be responding to texts, etc. on their phone.

Given what we know about the teenage brain, teens should not be given free reign when it comes to social media access. According to the American Academy of Pediatrics (2011), there are a number of risks to teenagers being online too much and using social media. The risks are:

- **Being Influenced by Advertising** – Advertisements online target teens encouraging them to buy certain things, behave certain ways, and believe specific things. Behavior and belief ads are powerful influences during the teenage years.

- **Posting Personal Information** – Posting too much personal information in personal profiles (school names and schedules, trips or vacations, addresses, phone numbers, etc.) puts teenagers and their families at risk. Teenagers don't realize how predators behave, what they are after, and how they use posted information to get it.

- **Posting False Information** – Everyone wants people to think they have a great life. Some even post false information about themselves (jobs, relationships, traveling, etc.) leading others to think they are something they are not. Their online self is far cooler or more interesting than their real self.

- **Posting Inappropriate Information** – Sometimes it's hard for teens to decide what is and isn't appropriate. Teenage girls post photos of themselves looking seductive, while boys post photos of themselves looking cool and aloof (Kapidzic & Herring, 2011). Posting inappropriate information whether it's sexual, violent, or socially provocative may affect their future. Employers and others check online to get a glimpse of who they are hiring. Teens don't always realize that what they post online never goes away and can come back to haunt them.

- **Experiencing Facebook Depression** – Spending too much time on social media sites is what is called Facebook depression and it comes from coveting the relationships, things, and lives of others. Comparing your life to another's or self-comparison with unattainable images is the death of happiness. Nobody's real life is as fabulous as it appears online.

- **Sexting** – Many of today's teens are sending, receiving, or forwarding sexually explicit messages, images, or videos. About 20% of teens have posted nude or semi-nude photos or videos of themselves (Schurgin Okeefe, Clarke-Pearson, & Council on Communications and Media, 2011). Many teens are looking for love in all the wrong places without being able to assess real risk.

- **Experiencing Cyberbullying** – Whether they are sharing false, embarrassing, or hostile information about another person online or having somebody posting about them, they are experiencing cyberbullying. Some teens aren't aware that they are the bully or are participating in bullying behavior online. Also, many teens don't know what to do when they are cyberbullied. The best way to fight cyberbullying is to get off social media and not respond.

- **Exposure to Inappropriate Content** – It is far too easy for teenagers to have access to pornography online and to hide it from their parents. Predators create fake accounts to reach out to adolescents and far too many of them respond to the bait.

The teen years are about fitting in and looking for where and how they fit in. It is also when they begin to look for a purpose. Ninety-two percent of teens report going on social media daily and 24% say they are nearly always connected (Seidman, 2016). Many use social media postings to find support and boost their self-esteem and since they haven't yet determined who they are, who they want to be, or what their purpose is, they may be allowing social media feedback to affect the development of self and purpose; giving the online feedback too much credence. In a study by Burrow and Rainone (as cited in Seidman, 2016) it was found that if teens feel a sense of purpose they are less affected by social media approval.

Girls and boys use social media in different ways. Lenhart and Madden (as cited in Herring and Kapidzic, 2015) point out that girls are more likely to focus on friendships, posting photos of themselves and their friends, or themselves with their friends. They also point out that boys are more likely to post on sports and humor or sometimes politics. Research shows that children, preteens, and teenagers are using massive amounts of media and those with more screen time have been shown to have increased obesity, reduced physical activity, and decreased health (Rosen et al., 2014). Furthermore, the more time spent online, the less time people spend learning about making and keeping relationships with real people.

Behavior

Teenagers "have less ability to process negative information than adults, so they're less inclined not to do something risky, and less likely to learn from their mistakes than adults" (Jensen, 2015). "The chief predictor of adolescent behavior is not the perception of the risk, but the anticipation of the reward despite the risk" (Jensen, 2015). This, and the fact that they are also hyped up on emotion, explains their unconcern for sexual activity. While the idea of *Just Say No* is a good one, it is eclipsed by the influence of society, their peers, emotion, and raging hormones. When you ask them, "What were you thinking?" It's not that they weren't thinking, it's that the part of their brain that tells them something might not be the best idea is still under construction. Sometimes teenage behavior can be impulsive and sometimes it only seems impulsive for our place of brain maturity.

In their desire to be adults and as teens begin to look more mature sexually, they may allow themselves to be exposed to social situations they may not be ready to handle. Encourage parents and students to talk about these possibilities and have a "rescue" plan in place to help relieve anxiety and keep them safe. Teenage parties can include drugs, alcohol, and the pressure to participate in sexual activity. Give them an out!

So, if giving teens a lot of freedom and telling them not to do something doesn't have much influence with them, what is the answer? While it may be hard on the adult's nerves and teens will often rail against it, it is far more beneficial to limit their exposure to risky situations (McNeely & Blanchard, 2009). It is okay to say, "No." It is okay for them to be angry, it won't last forever. Adults are not immune to this problem and there are examples of that in the Bible. King David, a man after God's own heart, made some very bad choices and his brain was fully mature. Adults cheat on their spouses, take drugs, and gamble away their family's money with fully mature brains. Talk to teens about it. What is the difference between not being able to assess the risk and ignoring it?

Most conflicts between teenagers and adults surround their desire to be independent. With their limited world experience and push to be independent, they want to make their own choices. They will test the rules and limits more than ever before. They will talk back, they will not want to tell you where they are going or who they are with, they will tell you that you don't understand, they will debate the rules with you because they think they know better. All of these behaviors should be reminders that their frontal lobes are underdeveloped.

Teenagers need independence WITH responsibility. Expect them to own their behavior and hold them accountable for their choices and behaviors. If they are not respectful to adults or peers it's acceptable to pull them out of class for a very brief chat about how you expect them to behave. Practice restoration and expect them to apologize when necessary and fix things when broken. I once told a student that his behavior was bothering people. He looked around the room and said nobody was bothered. I said, "I am people too."

I had two posters that I used regularly in my classrooms depending on the respect level of the class: 1) Respect Learning (Be on time and prepared, don't disrupt class, no electronic devices, no food/drink without permission), Respect Property (No gum under tables or chairs, don't sit on tables, don't write on tables), Respect People (Speak to and treat each other well, don't borrow without asking, keep your hands to yourself, use appropriate language), and 2) Live as a Friend, Learn as a Disciple, 3) Love as a Servant, and Lead as a Guide. Sometimes students need things to be straight forward. Sometimes a conversation about what it means to Live as a Friend, Learn as a Disciple, Love as a Servant, and Lead as a Guide is enough.

Teenagers are fun to teach! They have a great sense of humor and most enjoy sarcasm as long as it's not directed at them or used to make them feel stupid or inferior. Roll your eyes at the irony of the world, not them. Laugh with them!

CHAPTER 14

High School Bible Inquiry

Bible Inquiry is far more interesting and engaging than Bible study. Bible study is about sitting in a group, listening and answering a few questions. As was mentioned in the middle school chapter, Bible Inquiry is about probing for the truth, seeking to learn through queries or questions, investigating, and discussing. To participate in Bible Inquiry is not to sit and listen. It's to dig and discover! This requires the ability to craft questions in a way that requires more than obvious answers and includes the expectation that kids will discuss, debate, and grow.

When looking at typical published curriculums or lessons for high school, you'll see some full of activity and little meaning and some with a lot of meaning, text or lecture, and little or no activity. They need both.

When evaluating whether or not to use a curriculum for your high school you there are a few things to stay away from:

1) **Telling them what to think.** If you want to impact a teenager, ask them what they think and give them something to think about instead of telling them what to think. When we tell them what to think we challenge their autonomy and aren't giving them the opportunity to solidify their own thoughts and feelings which is shallow learning and does not effect change.

2) **Telling them how to live.** The whole world is constantly giving messages contrary to the Bible. If you want to impress teenagers, let them discuss and discover why doing something contrary to God's word will have negative consequences in their lives. Teens know they shouldn't do drugs or have sex, but they don't always understand the risks. They need to talk about it with their peers who have greater influence on them at this age.

3) **Telling them what the Bible says** or means before they have a chance to dig in and figure it out for themselves. "Read Matthew

5:14-16. In these verses, Jesus is telling us…" and then have them fill in the blank. Try, what is Jesus telling us in these verses and what is written to make you think that?

4) **Lecture, lecture, lecture.** You know there's a problem when you get to page 23 and haven't seen a question. Stay away from studies where the leader talks more than the kids search or discuss. Talking isn't teaching and hearing isn't learning.

5) **Discussion killing questions.** All questions are not created equal. Questions that have yes/no answers, one word answers, or don't lead anywhere, also don't lead to discussion or promote a question-asking atmosphere.

When we talk about behavior with teenagers, our lessons become very law oriented: don't do drugs, don't have sex, do read the Bible, and do go to church, but remember that Jesus loves you and we aren't saved based on our behavior. Again, our goal should be to get them in the word, have the hard discussions, and allow them to ask challenging questions. We pray that as they continue to grow (and their frontal lobes mature) they will continue to ask questions and seek answers in the word.

Typical vs. Bible Inquiry Lesson

It can be a challenge to create a Bible Inquiry lesson from a typical high school curriculum. Many of them have object lessons and crafts more suited to younger kids; it is also difficult to break the habit of telling instead of helping kids discover and challenging them. On the left below is a breakdown of a typical published high school lesson (A Mighty Wonder: Beginning of Time, 2019) about creation and on the right, suggestions to make it Bible Inquiry.

Beginning of Time Lesson	Bible Inquiry Suggestions
Creation	Genesis 1:1-2:3
What does the account of creation tell you about God? DISCUSSION POINT: • God is powerful • God is orderly • God is creative • God is loving	After reading the scripture once, hand out a worksheet and ask students to find 4 things that tell them about God and to list the verse(s) to support it. After they have done this talk about the 4 they listed and others they may have come up with.
Read and visualize what God made each day. When time is up, gather everyone together to share their work. DISCUSSION POINT: Day 1… Day 2… etc.	Use the Think Tank discussion method (next chapter) to get students to respond to the listed statements that show intelligent design. If it helps, choose one side to argue the nonbiblical side. OR

What questions do you think people have about the creation of the world? (COMMENT: Unless the goal is to have them memorize what was created each day, by high school, students have most likely drawn the days of creation many times and sharing their drawings or words takes valuable time away from discussion. The question is good, but having it where it is implies that the questions people might have would be about what was created each day.)	Use the Ultimate Top 3 or 5 to get students to think from the perspective of non-Christians. Look at the passage again. Were all 3 persons of God present when the universe was created? How do you know?
How do we know God really created the universe? DISCUSSION POINT: Many scientific facts of planet Earth point to a divine designer. When you look at the complex workings of our universe, the theory of evolution is even more unbelievable.	CONCLUSION: In the beginning, God created the heavens and the earth. Genesis 1:1

Note: A discussion point is not the same as a question. It is a statement and is usually read aloud. It doesn't give participants anything to discuss and the goal in every youth Bible study should be to get the kids thinking: What is the problem? What does the world think? What does the Bible say? What do I think? How does this strengthen my faith?

Note: A very important part of Bible Inquiry is the questions asked. Good questions enhance discussion and bad questions kill it. Chapter 18 on questions is at the end of the book and applies to both high schoolers and adults. It is called GOOD QUESTIONS and is on page 137.

Tips for Teaching High School

Some of the information and tips in the middle school chapter will also apply to high school and more in-depth ideas are in the next chapter. Miscellaneous tips for teaching high school are:

- Encourage healthy, respectful debate by setting rules of engagement. The first of these is to respect each other. Everybody needs to feel safe in speaking their thoughts.
- Before correcting their logic, listen and acknowledge what they say and then model your logic for them.
- Ask how they arrived at their conclusion.
- Take them through the risks of certain behaviors through questions.
- Ask open-ended questions: How do you think…?

- Continue developing deeper conversations about why people believe what they do and why they behave the way they do.
- Continue more complex moral or ethical dilemmas and looking at the people and stories of the Bible from different perspectives. What would you do if you were in their situation?
- From this period through adulthood students should be allowed to struggle with beliefs and come to with their own conclusions... with your guidance. Challenge their thinking and encourage them to include Biblical support for doctrinal issues.
- Talk about what they post online and why they do it in comparison to what God thinks about them.

CHAPTER 14

High School Discussion

Teaching teens can be intimidating to some people, but it's not hard if you have some understanding of their world. That's why it's important to understand what's going on in their brains and where they are socially, emotionally, and cognitively. Most youth Bible studies seem to either be heavy on the lecture and light on meaningful interaction or heavy on the interaction, but light on the content. We're looking for a balance. Including videos and fancy graphics or games and posting ideas for social media are not the important part of a curriculum or Bible study. Teenagers don't come to Bible study because you use social media. They come if they leave feeling better about themselves and life and believing they've been told the truth. The best way to get them to the truth is to do Bible Inquiry with dynamic discussion.

Teenagers are in the midst of deciding who they are or want to be and what they believe; they should have enough Bible education that they can discuss what they know and be able to communicate how they feel about it. They are searching for the truth so they can decide for themselves what to believe. Our goal should be to get them into the Bible where they will find the truth, and challenge them to compare the messages they get from society to the message of the gospel and the love of Jesus. It's not about cool videos and social media. It's not about fun and games. It's about a meaningful interaction with God's word.

Facilitating Teen Discussion

When facilitating discussions with teenagers it's important to remember that their brains are not fully developed, their bodies are being overrun by hormones, they are sensitive to the perceptions of the opposite sex, and they have the life experience of a 15-18 year old. That's not a lot of experience. High school students, while they're sure they know so much more, have a limited world view. Try not to forget this when considering their responses and when trying to explain things.

For example, once I had a mom come to talk to me about her son, my high school student. Her son disagreed with me about one of my rules and she explained that he had a strong sense of fairness and justice. He thought I was being unfair. I reminded her that his sense of justice was from a 16 year old viewpoint, not an experienced teacher and I explained the situation from the broader perspective. A teacher considers one student, the whole class, how something might affect other classes, and how the decision will affect people in the long run when making a decision. A high school student primarily considers him/herself and his/her friends.

A nice way to respond to comments where some guidance or correction is necessary is to model your decision making process aloud while you come to a logical conclusion (APA, 2002). Also, try repeating what's already been said to see if they see where the logic fails such as, "Here's what I've heard so far… is that right?"

Discussion Don'ts

Facilitating discussion is an art (Langhoff, 2014). It depends on good timing and practiced skills. Effective discussion can provide a number of positive interactions between students and the teacher, and between students and the material. It also provides feedback and supports a higher level of thinking that helps develop values and change attitudes (Langhoff, 2014). Discussion allows students to participate in their learning, and gives them a chance to hear and share different viewpoints (Schurr, 1995).

Sometimes getting a discussion started or keeping it going can be dependent on the facilitator, especially when the culture of the class has been passive. Following are facilitator tips:

Atmosphere – Create an atmosphere where people feel comfortable sharing. Be careful when using sarcasm. Not everybody understands it. Also, make sure people understand that discussion is give and take, and shouting at people won't get them to agree with you. Discussion is not about verbally bullying people into agreement. We listen, respond respectfully, and listen more.

Small Groups – Don't let teens choose their own small groups. They choose the same people (their friends) all the time and end up not getting much done. Choose groups randomly every week using craft sticks with everyone's name on them. If they know you're going to count off, they'll put themselves in the order that puts them with their friends.

Time to Respond – One of the things facilitators do without realizing it is rush. Waiting for a response can be difficult. Time seems to move very slowly when you ask a question and they sit there looking at you or the floor. They're usually afraid they'll say the wrong thing in front of everyone, so give them time to think and respond. If the teacher jumps in with a response, students will wait until that happens every time which will stifle the discussion.

Encourage Without Giving Too Much – When facilitators want to encourage students they often give away too much in their hint. Sometimes they use the fill-in-the-blank method by starting an answer and hoping they can finish it by coming up with the last word or they give too much of a hint. Sometimes they give an answer so close they can't possibly miss it. While the intention is good, this method does not help discussion.

Judge a Response – Try not to tell students directly that they're wrong. Tell them they are close, ask if they have more to offer, tell them they are partly right, or make a habit of making a game show noise. Be careful of showing disapproval with facial expressions and other body language. You would be surprised what students will pick up from body language.

Speak Less – Sometimes it's easy to forget you're facilitating and get involved in the conversation to the point that you take over to prove your point. You might even slip into lecture mode. The point of discussion is to find out what they know/believe in case they need some guidance or more information. Guide them by asking more questions, not directly sharing your opinion. When you speak you should be giving them facts (in this case Biblical or historical information) to think about or asking questions.

Give Your Opinion at the End – If you state your opinion too early, they will agree with you and the discussion will be over. Try to get them to come to a conclusion without directly or indirectly stating your opinion until the end.

Want to Hear More? – There are a number of phrases that will help get positive responses when students aren't getting the point. Ask another question to get them to think a little more deeply.

- Why do you think that?
- I need help clarifying. Can you give me an example?
- What do you mean by…?
- I'd like to hear more about that.
- What about…?
- Does anybody else have something to add?

Adolescent Discussion Starters

Sometimes getting started is tough because it's a tough group. The same vocal students may consistently respond, the group looks at you as if you don't speak their language, or they may be reasonably sure you'll answer your own questions if they wait long enough. When that happens, try to get them moving with one of the following options:

A Beanbag – Start by asking a simple nonthreatening question that any student can answer and toss a beanbag to a student to respond. You can have them toss it back to you or to another student to respond to the same question or the next question. Increase the depth of the questions as the beanbag is tossed around and students will start sharing. Don't be surprised if at one point somebody says, "Throw it to me!" because they have something to share. If they start talking over each other remind them that the person with the beanbag is the speaker and everyone else listens and thinks. If you feel they're up to a challenge you may even toss the beanbag before you ask the question.

Agree, Disagree, Don't Know—Put AGREE, DISAGREE and DON'T KNOW signs up around the room and have students respond to a statement by standing under a sign. Give them a moment to think, but don't let them talk to their friends before they move and don't forget to ask why they disagree or agree while they're standing under the sign. To challenge them, see if they can change the minds of the others to their opinion and ask anybody who changes their mind why they changed it.

Continuum – Similar to the agree/disagree signs, this strategy uses a continuum from one to five or one to ten along a wall. Students respond to how strongly they agree or disagree about a statement. Once they pick a number, have them write on a piece of paper why they chose it. After some information or discussion give everybody a chance to move and if they do, write down that reason or verbally explain.

Fist-to-Five – Similar to the continuum, this strategy uses a fist as zero or "I completely disagree" and the whole hand (all five fingers) or "I completely agree" as the 1 to 5 scale of agreement. Students need to close their eyes so they don't see how others respond. Write down how students responded and put them in groups to discuss why they responded the way they did. Possible questions for each group:

- Why do you disagree so strongly?
- Why do you agree so strongly?
- Why are you middle of the road?

Agree/Disagree, Continuum, Fist-to-Five are great when starting with common societal beliefs students may have bought into. The goal for these discussion starters is not only to talk about what kids believe, but to start the conversation. The goal is to talk about what God wants for our lives and why, so it's important not to get stuck on the discussion starter and to move on to God's Word. Remember we want to know what they're thinking before we find out what God says about it.

All of these strategies can be used to get a specific conversation started. Don't be as concerned about whether or not they agree or disagree as *why* they agree or disagree. One of the goals of a discussion is to help students refine and communicate what they think or believe. We want to give them the opportunity to develop their own thoughts, opinions, and feelings based on what they have learned. However, they are young and again, their logic may be off, so let them be challenged and see if they figure it out for themselves before you jump in and correct. There's nothing better than watching the wheels turn in the heads of teenagers as they rationalize and realize things they didn't before. It's after great discussion that they talk about it later that week.

Adolescent Discussion Strategies

Discussion needs to be structured and facilitated. I can't say enough that effective discussion is NOT the teacher/leader talking and asking questions while a few outspoken students respond. The leader's job is to listen, observe, and consider next steps while students talk. Here are a few ways to get more out of your discussion:

#1: Ultimate Top 3 or 5

Have students work in groups to decide the top three or top five (depending on the size of your group) reasons for something. Write significant questions or thoughtful statements about what you're going to talk about. Ask for the three most important reasons why something is true or the five most common idols in our culture, or any similar question.

Round 1 – Have groups discuss why their responses should be the ultimate top three or five. Take those responses to Round 2.

Round 2 – Put two groups together to determine the top 3 or 5 of their combined responses.

Round 3 – Put two of the bigger groups together until the large group has the ultimate top 3 or 5.

For example, if the topic is creation vs. evolution, have students write down as many answers as they can think of to the question: What makes people think God did not create the universe? The next question: What makes people think evolution is true? When they get each question pared down to the top 3 they should discuss those answers and how they might respond to them.

#2: Gallery Walk

This will most likely take more than one week or one lesson. Write significant questions or thoughtful statements about what you're going to talk about on large sticky notes and place them around the room. The sticky notes are to help start discussion, so make sure you ask good questions or make good statements that help guide students to your goals. Remember that the goal is to have discussion, not to write sticky notes.

Round 1 – Give each student a few small sticky notes. It doesn't matter what color they are. Have small groups travel around the room reading the questions or statements and responding to them on their sticky notes. Post them on the wall next to the question/statement. Students can ask questions or make comments about what they read.

Round 2 – Have students walk around the room again and put a hash mark on questions or comments students want to have answered or want to talk more about. If they have follow-up questions they can add them then too.

The facilitator then walks around the room and uses the students' comments and questions to help guide the discussion. Because this is a Bible study, we need to put the Bible in it. When students are done walking around the gallery, hand out a variety of verses for them to look up.

For example, if you're talking about Holy Communion your questions or statements might be :

- What would you tell your younger sister who wants to go to her friend's non-denominational church and take communion?
- What's the problem with participating in communion at a church that doesn't believe what I do?
- What would you tell a friend who came to church with you about going up for communion?
- It doesn't matter what other churches believe, God knows what I believe.
- It doesn't matter if a non-believer takes communion. It won't be the same for him.
- Do you have to take communion with a pastor in a church?

Notice how the questions are not out of a catechism, but more related to real life issues. Students then walk around the room putting up comments and questions; and go around again putting up hash marks. The facilitator then hands out a list of Bible verses and has students write down what each one means. Below are two examples among many.

Luke 21:33	My word will never pass away
Acts 2:42	Devoted to teaching, fellowship, breaking of bread, prayers

The facilitator then takes each question and what students added and together they go through the questions and verses to come to an answer.

#3: Bring Your Catechism and Bible

Have students sit in groups or teams of 3 or 4 and have each group choose a name (you can give them a number, but kids, you know, like to name their groups). They are going to respond to some questions that a non-believer might ask. Have the questions prepared in advance and have them in a can or jar or hat so you can pull them out randomly. Give each group one question that they will ask another group. In their final response, each group is required to have at least two Bible verses to support their response. They may discover that the questions and answers in the back of the catechism are very helpful.

Round 1 – Each group receives a question and spends time coming up with a good answer. It MUST be in their own words and have two supporting Bible verses.

Some questions might be:

- Why doesn't the church down the street baptize babies?
- Why are babies baptized if they haven't sinned yet?
- If God is love, what's wrong with being gay?
- Why doesn't God like gay people?
- Why doesn't your church have women pastors?
- Why can't my friends go to communion with me?
- If we're all saved then why do we need to follow the commandments?
- Why do Catholics confess to a priest and we don't?
- If God knows everything, why do we have to confess our sins at all?
- Why should I pray?

If you want to challenge them, do the same thing with questions atheists ask that can be found online in the Skeptics Annotated Bible. Give 5-10 minutes for students to come up with an answer for their question.

Round 2 – After each group gives their answer, let the other groups add points or ideas to their answer.

Round 3 – Let each group pick a different question and answer it based on what they learned.

#4: Paper Airplanes

As you go over what you're studying, prepare 5-10 questions or statements that you think will get the students talking. Remember that you ask questions to find out what they know/believe, to challenge their beliefs, or to make them think.

For example, if you're talking about forgiveness a statement might be: Give an example of something that would be hard to forgive. A question might be: Why is it important that you forgive someone for that unforgiveable offense? Have students respond, fold it into a simple paper airplane and fly it either to the teacher or into the middle of the room.

#5: Think Tank

A card table and four chairs sit in the middle of the room. This is the Think Tank. Four students sit at the table and the remaining students sit around the table. On the back of each chair is a card that has an A, B, C, and D taped to it. If you have a large number of students you'll want to break them up into groups and have more than one Think Tank.

The goal of this exercise is to have students in the Think Tank discuss statements surrounding a provided topic. All students need to have something to write with and paper. (I usually cut copy paper into fourths.) The students around the room are on team A, B, C, or D, or they sit behind their person at the table. They are to provide questions or information to the one in the seat to defend their position or comments, refute the statement, or challenge the other three sitting at the table. After a chosen amount of time, no more than 10 minutes, the people sitting at the table rotate and a new statement or question is chosen until everyone has had a chance to sit at the table.

Students are asked to bring their Bibles, Small Catechisms, and their brains. Instead of giving them general topics, they are given challenge statements. Reasons and or examples must be given for what they believe. If they're going to use the Bible, they have to provide a reference so they might want a Bible with a concordance. It is important for the teacher to monitor the statements made in case the discussion goes off the rails and students end up debating untruths. I recommend having a bell or buzzer and when somebody says something that isn't true the bell is rung. If you want to make it more of a competition, give points to each team for every statement they make and take points away from the team every time you have to ring the bell on them.

For example, everybody is in their appropriate seats and everyone has paper and pencil and their reference materials. The teacher or leader lays down a piece of paper and written in large print is the phrase, "God created evil." Go! If students hesitate, urge them to respond by asking, "Yes or no? Did he or didn't he? Why do you think so?" Below are some statements and/or questions to get you started:

Good God – Bad World
God doesn't exist because of the evil in the world.
Why would a good God allow so much evil?
Evil's existence helps the world find God.
The world is full of evil because God is testing us.
God should stop evil in the world.
God is Love
Love is accepting everything someone does, no matter what.
Love is accepting everyone no matter what.
If God loves everyone then everyone will be in heaven.
How is discipline considered love?
Does God forgive people who hate him?

God's Law
The law is mean and nobody needs it.
If we're forgiven the law doesn't matter.
The law leads people to the gospel.
I can't follow the law, so why try?
I don't have to follow the law to be a good Christian.
Baptism
Baptism saves you. That's all you need.
If you're baptized, how can you lose your faith?
Baptizing babies is wrong.
Repentance
If I don't repent I won't go to heaven.
My sins are forgiven, I don't need to repent.
Creation
Evolution and creation can fit together.
God's days are longer than our days.
Evolution makes more sense than creation.
Believing God created the world takes more faith than evolution.
Evolution has been proven.
Holy Communion
The Lord's Supper is something everyone should be allowed to take.
Telling people they can't take communion at your church is mean.
I can take communion at my friend's church.
The Lord's Supper is something we can do without thinking. Just do it!
The 10 Commandments
The hardest commandment to keep is...
The easiest commandment to keep is...
Breaking the commandments really has no effect on my life.
There are no consequences for not following God's law

PART V

WISDOM STAGE
Adults

The Wisdom Stage is the time of adulthood. It begins in the middle twenties and encompass the rest of life. By the time we're adults we've forgotten much of what we learned as children, especially in confirmation. By now the brain has fully matured, we know the stories, have thought about them, learned from them and have finally reached the point of wisdom. We're done! Not at all. The truly wise know that where faith is concerned, learning only ends once we are in the presence of the Lord. As we read the same stories and passages over and over God continues to reveal new truths to us. Though life gets busy and more challenging, adults need and want to learn more about their Savior. Wisdom comes from above, true peace comes from above, and the more we study scripture, the wiser we become. As we are conformed to the likeness of Christ we become less weary, less afraid, less stressed, and more trusting, more peaceful, and filled with more joy. To get there we need to struggle with God's Word.

> But the wisdom from above is first pure, then peaceable, gentle, open to reason, full of mercy and good fruits, impartial and sincere. James 3:17 ESV

CHAPTER 15

Adults

Though it may not always seem that way, adults want to learn more about God, His Word, and their faith. They do! They also have a lot of questions and misunderstandings. Many may have ideas that do not fit with the teachings of the Bible, especially with all the inaccurate information floating around the internet. For many of them it's been 20-50 years since their confirmation and they haven't continued studying. Far more members do not know what the church they attend teaches than any pastor wants to acknowledge..

In the church, for the last 100+ years, the culture of adult Bible study in most congregations has not changed. It is primarily a culture of passivity and people have become comfortable with that. There is nearly always coffee, often treats, and usually not a lot of participation expected, if any. Too often it's sitting and listening. There will be a few questions asked, but they are not challenging and participation is optional. A few regulars will respond, but nobody will have to speak, feel uncomfortable, or have their beliefs challenged. Unfortunately, and contrary to this tradition, telling is not teaching, and hearing is not learning.

Mark Blanke, in the Journal of Lutheran Mission (2016), reported that about 21% of adult members participate in adult learning in the church. Why is adult Bible study attendance so poor? There are a number of theories out there. My theory is that it's because adult Bible study is a challenge to attend. Nobody trains those who teach adults in the church. The way adults are taught in the church is by lecture. We hear a sermon and then go to Bible study for a longer sermon. This is what the Bible says and this is what you should believe, we are told. I had one pastor who read to us from the Book of Concord for 45 minutes and wondered why people stopped coming. Why has adult education not changed in all this time?

There are most likely many reasons and among them somewhere could be any of these:

- Pastors haven't been taught how to facilitate discussion well.
- Pastors think they teach well.
- Pastors haven't been taught the difference between good questions (those that require thought) and bad questions (those that require no thought).
- Pastors are afraid they won't be able to answer some questions people will ask.
- People think that if their pastor is funny that he's a good teacher.
- People don't know what a good class is because they've never attended one.

Blanke (2016) also reports that 57% of pastors have had no college coursework in education or teaching other than one required course that does not focus on the methodology of teaching adolescents or adults. Furthermore, a similar percentage has not taken continuing education in this area. Perhaps that is because there is little to be had. Yet, they also report that about 25% of their time is spent in educational duties (Blanke, 2016).

Adults and Learning

From what we learned earlier about how the brain learns, we know that a young brain is shaped by experience, and the teenage brain is ripe for learning, but that does not mean that the adult brain does not learn. It may happen more slowly than when we are young, but adult brains are shaped by experience too (Jensen, 2015). The difference is that our frontal lobe, which is inhibitory, is in full function.

Teaching adults is not the same as teaching children or adolescents with regard to approach and methodology. Adults take charge of their lives, make their own decisions, and decide whether or not to participate in educational opportunities; they have also accumulated life experience and knowledge (Kamp, 2011). While children are required to do what their parents choose, adults direct themselves. How we educate adults makes a difference as to their attendance and retention. Sometimes people have the attitude that adults should go to Bible study whether they enjoy it or not and perhaps they should because it's good for them, but as adults they don't have to. They also don't have to eat healthy or exercise.

Every book of the Bible is full of compelling information and God's truth. It's not even remotely boring stuff, but sometimes it's presented that way. Like with most things, it's not WHAT you teach - it's HOW you teach that makes the greatest difference. Adults want to believe that what they are taught is relevant and useful, but sometimes we teach it as if we don't believe that it is.

Adults are typically motivated to attend Bible study for these reasons (in no special order) (adapted from Lieb, 1991):

- **Social Relationships** – to get together and feel connected with friends and/or make new friends. People enjoy opportunities to be together and especially enjoy learning with friends.

- **External Expectations** – to comply with instructions made by someone else. Sometimes it's required for a job, but with Bible study it may be a spouse's request.

- **Social Welfare** – to improve their ability to serve mankind. Sometimes in order to serve in an area such as Stephen Ministry or other helping ministry specific education is required. Sometimes in order to feel competent at outreach people want to know as much as possible about the Bible. And sometimes we know that the more we study God's Word the greater desire we have to be like Jesus and serve.

- **Escape/Stimulation** – to provide a break in the routine of home or work. Sometimes people need a break from life and there's no better way to spend that time than in the Word.

- **Cognitive Interest** – to learn for the sake of growing and learning more about their Savior.

Of course, where adult Bible study is concerned, we hope everybody is coming to learn more about their Savior, develop a closer relationship with Him, and to grow their faith.

Multiple Ages

A major challenge when teaching adult Bible study is that adults range in age from 18 through 80+ years old and are in different stages of life. This means they have different needs as learners. Some are still searching for identity and purpose, some are new to Bible study and some have been studying the Bible for over 50 years. Also, some are in the building stage of life, marrying and building careers and family, others have settled down, and many have reached the age of life acceptance; they accept what life is or has been, that it has an end, and realize what is most important to them.

The common thread to having a multi-age class is that participants can learn from each other's experience. Being young doesn't mean you have no insight to share and being old doesn't mean you know it all. It's the same the other way. Being old doesn't mean you have nothing to share and being young doesn't mean you know it all. With proper respect for all who attend they can learn from each other. Nobody has the corner on biblical insight.

The most wonderful thing about the Bible is, if it's taught in a meaningful way, everyone can learn something new from every passage.

Seating & Class Size

Two other challenges of Adult Bible Study are seating and varying class sizes. Adult classes are held in classrooms, fellowship halls, and even the sanctuary. Class sizes range from a few to a hundred or more. How do you discuss in these situations?

Most churches have either rectangular or circular tables that seat eight. Each table can easily become a discussion group if people sit together. When I teach adults I ask people to move to another table if they're sitting alone. Some don't want to and then find they have nobody to discuss the questions with, but it's okay to ask people to move. It's a little more difficult if people are sitting in rows, and especially if they are in pews. Pews cannot be turned around so people can face each other. If the only place you can have adult Bible study is the sanctuary, you may need to get creative. Try smaller groups, two or three in front, two or three in back, and those in front will need to turn a bit. Needless to say, the sanctuary is great for a sermon, but not so much for a discussion

People are creatures of habit. Families all at one table don't always create a diverse group. Once the class gets used to discussing you can mix up the regular groups. When you have dynamic discussion and people get excited about what they're learning, they will look forward to sitting with other people.

Using Slides

If you are going to use slides to share material, make sure that there aren't too many or too few words on each slide. Remember that we think in pictures so if you're going to talk about a region, use a map. If you're going to talk about culture, use pictures. For words try using the 5/5/5 rule: No more than 5 words per line, 5 lines per slide, and 5 text-heavy slides in a row. Don't talk while people are writing and they shouldn't need to write down every word on every slide, but they should have a handout to take notes. Do NOT choose unreadable fonts and background colors. Dark text on a white background or white text on a dark gray or black background is easiest to read. Slide creation tips:

- Make sure slides can be easily read from the back of the room.
- A 24 point font is the smallest you should use.
- Add no more than five bullet points to each slide.
- Use more photos and less text.
- Avoid excessive verbiage.
- Be careful of being redundant.

- Be consistent with how you word things.
- NEVER read your slides as you present.

A lot of people will create slides and make copies of them to hand them out to class so people can take notes. That's a good idea if you expect people to take notes of your lecture. The goal of slides, however, should be to enhance what you're saying. The goal of Bible study is to get people into the word so slides need to be used to that end.

CHAPTER 16

Adult Bible Inquiry

It's as important to have a plan when teaching adults as it is when teaching kids. Some people use slides to help them plan. They put a lot of information on slides and then read the slides. Sometimes they have lists of Bible verses that they may have on slides so that nobody needs to have a Bible or handouts. When pressed for time it's the Bible verses that are often the first thing scratched because it takes so long for people to find and read them. The pastor or leader may summarize them instead. The reality of teaching Bible study is that to do it right it takes more time than you think. Why? Because what we really want is people in the Bible, talking to each other and asking questions, which means you'll also need time to answer their questions. It's so much more convenient to tell them what you want them to know through a lecture, but keep in mind how quickly they will forget what you say. A better way to think of Bible study is as Bible Inquiry. Bible Inquiry is about probing for the truth, seeking to learn through queries or questions, and investigating. To participate in Bible Inquiry is not to sit and listen. It's to delve and explore!

How the class is organized helps immensely. There are three main categories of adult Bible Inquiry:

- Discuss a **church topic**: baptism, Holy Communion, prayer, Lord's Prayer, forgiveness, etc.
- Study a book or passage of **scripture**: look for terms, themes, connections, etc.
- Address a **social problem**: gay marriage, transgenderism, abortion, etc.

Each category has a specific pedagogical model, however, the basic outline is: what does the world say, what does the Bible say, what do you think? When studying scripture, however, we don't care what the world says; we jump right in to see what God says.

Class Set Up

The standard set-up is for people to sit around tables so that everyone faces front. Nobody wants their back to the leader. This is fine as long as nobody is sitting alone. It may feel awkward, but if anybody is sitting by themselves at a table, ask them to move so they have somebody to talk to. Remind everyone that this is a class where they're allowed and encouraged to talk to their neighbors and share answers.

Make sure there is paper (try copy paper cut in fourths) and pens/pencils on each table. Also, have a question jar of some kind so that people can write down questions they have at the beginning of class and any they may come up with during class. Tell them you *will* get to every question.

Use a handout! Make sure everybody has a Bible. They're going to need one. There's an example for each of these models. Writing things down helps people remember them and it'll save time if you help them organize their thoughts. Their directions are to work together to get as much information about the who, what, where, when, and how about baptism from the Bible as they can and write their notes on the handout to be used later. Always put the list of Bible verses on the handout with room for them to make notes. They don't all have to look up every verse, but can work together and share answers.

Verse	Notes
Matthew 18:6, 28:19	

The job of the leader here is to wait and walk around the room while they do this. This made my pastor husband very uncomfortable as he was used to doing most of the talking. He was amazed that at every table people were talking! If there are some groups that seem to be sitting together, but working independently, stop and ask what they're finding. Encourage them to talk to each other or they won't get to all of them.

Church Topic: Baptism

The first category of Bible Inquiry is a church topic. When teaching about a church topic such as baptism or forgiveness, the first thing you want to know is what everybody knows or thinks about it. A good way to find out is through the questions they ask. As they arrive ask them to write any questions they have about it on the quarter size paper. While you pass out the handout have them put their questions in the jar. Put the jar in a place where they can add questions as they come up and then you can officially start with prayer. The jar helps because that way questions can be submitted anonymously.

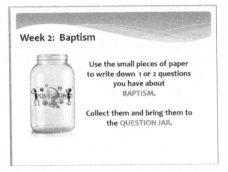

Ask the introductory question: What does the general public know/believe about baptism? What is it? Who does it? Why do they do it? Do people do it for different reasons? People feel more comfortable talking about what the general public knows than what they know. It's safer. Give them 3 or 4 minutes to do this. As they think, they may have questions.

Provide them a reason to talk. Sometimes I like to use scenarios. They help focus the discussion. The first item to encourage discussion is the first scenario:

> You have two daughters. They were both brought up in the Lutheran church, but married wonderful Christian men who are non-Lutherans and don't believe in infant baptism. One daughter has decided not to have her babies baptized. You disagree. What do you say to her?

Their task is to use the Bible verses to come up with how to respond to this scenario and the following scenarios. The handout looks like this with appropriate spacing.

What do you know/believe about the Baptism? _____

_____

Look at the Bible verses. What do they tell you about the who, what, when, where, and how of baptism? Make note of as much information as you can from each verse.

Verse	Notes
Matt. 18:6, 28:19	
Mark 10:13-15, 16:16	
Luke 1:15, 41-44	
Luke 7:30	
John 3:5-6	
Acts 2:38-41, 22:16	

Eph. 4:5, 5:26	
1 Cor. 4:1	
Col. 1:13-14	
Titus 3:5-8	

The second thing that encourages discussion is the list of pre-researched discussion questions. These questions will inspire other questions. Keep in mind that most likely not everyone in your class was raised Lutheran or confirmed Lutheran.

Some questions for this scenario might be:

- Why don't other Christian churches baptize babies?
- Why is it important that your grandchildren be baptized?
- What are the benefits of baptism?
- What would happen if your grandchild died and was not baptized?
- Can people be saved without being baptized?
- Does baptism guarantee faith or salvation?

Using the Bible verses, have the large group discussion about the scenario and the questions. Then go on to the next scenario:

> Your daughter continually tells you that they are dedicating the children who will choose to be baptized later when they're ready. You want your grandchildren baptized so badly that you secretly baptize them. What would or could the consequences be?

Some questions for this scenario might be:

- Why do other churches think people need to be ready to be baptized?
- What is the basic difference between what the beliefs of the churches?
- What does the Bible say about baptizing children without parental consent?
- What is the fear of not having them baptized?
- Do you think your pastor would baptize the baby?

Have the large group discussion about the scenario and the questions. Then go on to the next scenario:

> Your other daughter wants her children baptized, but her husband doesn't want it done in the Lutheran church. She asks you to do it now and they can re-do it when they get older in the other church. How do you respond? She has chosen some friends from the non-Lutheran church as sponsors. How would you respond to her choice of sponsors?

Some questions for this scenario might be:

- What's the harm in having two baptisms?
- What is the purpose of a sponsor?

Have the large group discussion about the scenario and the questions.

After each discussion of the scenarios the participants came up with more and more questions leading to more discussion. Taking the time for the discussion is extremely important to make sure everyone is on the same page with why we believe/teach what we do.

After each class, if you didn't have a chance to get to the question jar, take it home and make sure the questions came up in the discussion or if they still need to be addressed. If somebody asks something you didn't come across while you were preparing or something you can't answer, tell them you'll get back to them next week.

My husband and I team-taught this class. It was supposed to be a review or reminder of what was learned in confirmation about chosen topics. We had five weeks and thought we would get through five topics, but we only got through two and had to rush the second topic. There was such great discussion and so many questions that the class went on for two more weeks than planned! Afterward, people left notes about how much they loved the class and how much they felt they learned. Many asked when we would be teaching our next class. We used the same process when talking about the Lord's Supper. The key is to get them into the Word and start them discussing with prewritten questions. So many people have forgotten so much from when they learned it at 14 years old. They loved it and by the discussion alone we could see what they learned!

The purpose of the scenarios is to give them a jumping off point to start the process of inquiry. Then they do the Biblical research and come up with their own biblical answers. This teaches them that they don't have to have somebody standing in front of them telling them the answers. They can seek them on their own. The pastor or leader's job then is to keep the discussion focused and make sure nobody starts down the road of unbiblical truth. Discussing at tables also helps bring things up for discussion as a large group.

The Challenge with Scenarios

Sometimes there are issues with using scenarios. They don't work in every situation; they need to be crafted to fit and the questions need to fit the scenario.

In the past I attended a typical adult Bible study on forgiveness. The first three weeks were primarily a large group discussion. While there were many Bible verses on the screen, there was not much digging into scripture and a number of the same issues kept coming up. On the fourth week a scenario was introduced:

Mom fell and broke a hip and was in the hospital. The son previously promised his dad that he would take care of his mom, not putting her in a nursing home. The sister thought a nursing home was a good idea. There was conflict. The brother assumed he was right and the sister said he was stupid.

The questions that were to be discussed with the scenario in mind were questions that were posed in weeks 1 – 3 and were:

1. How have you contributed to this conflict? Who has been affected by your sinful thoughts, words, or actions?
2. In spite of your sinful nature, how does your heavenly Father view you and the person with whom you are in conflict?
3. In light of how your heavenly Father views you both, what is your worth to God? What is the other person's worth to God?
4. What comfort does your baptism give you in the midst of this struggle?
5. In Christ, we are called as new creatures to put away our "old self" and put on our "new self" in Christ. How can you put away your old self in this conflict? How can you put on your new self? What would your contrition and repentance look like?
6. Describe what material or substantive issues need to be resolved.
7. Identify what relational issues need to be reconciled in your conflict.
8. Write a prayer asking for God's help in resolving the material issues and reconciling with the other person.

What is wrong with this scenario and/or the questions, if anything? Think about them for a few moments. To focus your thoughts think about these questions:

- Do the scenario and questions reflect the topic?
- Do the questions connect to the scenario?
- Do the questions challenge the students in some way?

The scenario is about conflict and the questions are about conflict resolution. Forgiveness may or may not have anything to do with conflict or resolution. As was discussed in the previous weeks, we forgive because we are told to forgive as we are forgiven, not because we have resolved conflict and everything is warm and fuzzy again. Nothing is wrong with the scenario and the questions are good, but they aren't connected. The scenario isn't necessary to answer the questions.

What might a scenario about forgiveness be and what are the forgiveness issues in them?

- A woman's husband sexually abused his daughter. How does he ask for forgiveness? How does she give it? What about the rest of the family? Is it their business to forgive him?

- A child has an alcoholic or drug addicted parent. Does the child forgive if the parent is still an addict? What if the child doesn't feel he/she can forgive?
- A divorced couple had terrible fights and said horrible things to each other. If they both did it, do they need to forgive each other or is it a wash? What if one won't forgive?
- A teenager was driving down the highway when a man jumped in front of his car and was killed. How does he live with himself? Is there such a thing as forgiving yourself?
- A teenage girl has a friend who posted private information about her online. The whole school is talking about it. She can forgive, but the harassment at school continues. What does that kind of forgiveness look like?
- Somebody kidnaps and murders your child. How long might it take for you to forgive? How do you get to the place where you can forgive such a heinous act?
- A soldier sees the enemy using children as weapons. Can you forgive somebody and still hate them? Are there some people you shouldn't forgive? Does God forgive *everyone*? If not, who doesn't He forgive? If God doesn't forgive everyone, who do I not have to forgive? If God forgives everyone, why isn't everyone going to heaven?

Some deeper questions might be: How do you know when you need to forgive someone? If enough time has passed and you feel okay with somebody who hurt you, does that mean you've forgiven them? Are there other reasons, besides somebody directly hurting us, that we might need to forgive someone? If somebody hurt you so bad that you can't seem to bring yourself to forgive them? Where does repentance fall into all of this?

When developing scenarios and questions the goal needs to be kept in mind. If the point is to lead us to see that those who have hurt us as beloved sinners of God, it should be easier to forgive them. We are all broken. Some people are broken in different ways than others, and some perhaps more seriously, but knowing that should give us compassion toward them, allowing us to forgive them. We don't forgive them for them and we don't forgive them for God, we forgive them for us. This is an important part of the lesson. There are, however many questions that people struggle with regarding forgiveness and adults need to discuss them because they live them. Providing questions begins discussion which usually leads to more questions and further digging for biblical answers, which is exactly what we want: Bible Inquiry.

Scripture Study: Prodigal Son

The second category of Bible Inquiry is a scripture study. Obviously, studying a book or passage of scripture cannot be done using scenarios in the same way studying a topic can. It does, however, require some of the same steps in the process and can rarely be completed in one class period. There are four stages in a Bible Inquiry scripture study:

Introduction – where prior knowledge or information is shared.

Inquiry – where participants read in their groups and answer probing questions about the reading together.

Digging Deeper – looking at other passages and/or verses that connect to what is being studied.

Thinking it Through – deep application questions to be discussed as a large group.

Consider the Parable of the Prodigal Son. We are used to studying the Bible verse by verse, but sometimes looking with a broader lens helps when teaching. It will also help to look for other biblical connections. A pastor has far more education and knowledge about the Bible than most people do, especially when it comes to language use and historical/cultural context. They have been taught to do a very thorough biblical exegesis with the goal of finding the *una sensus literalis* or one true meaning of the text by taking into account culture, history, language, how words are used in the passage and elsewhere in the Bible. That kind of information is usually shared as a lecture.

Contrary to popular educational theory, lectures are not evil. They are often a great way to impart information and they can be dynamic and fun if the presenter is somewhat entertaining as long as they aren't too long. Entertaining or not, people do not remember what they hear for very long. A great way to work with biblical texts is to remember:

- Learn how to ask good questions. (See Chapter 18.) Good questions are a big deal. Challenge them!
- The class is not only about what the pastor or leader can tell them, it's about what they can learn, and again, hearing isn't learning.
- Provide time and tools for participants to participate in the process of inquiry. Use a handout!
- Provide a nonthreatening way for them to ask questions.
- Don't forget the application!

Below is a published sample study on Comfort (Weedon, 2009). (This example is also used in the chapter 18, about questions.) If you look at the text and the questions you can see that they are so straight forward that they can be very easily answered by simply looking at the text. There is no challenge, no application, and no deeper thought than what is written.

Read Matthew 6:19-34

1. **Why** does our Lord warn against focusing on earthly wealth?
2. **Why** is it impossible to serve (probably meaning, to worship) both God and Mammon (wealth)?
3. Dr. Kenneth Korby once said that "Wealth is served with the liturgy of anxiety." Based on this passage what do you think he meant?
4. **What** does our Lord seek to dispel in this passage?
5. **What** does our Lord seek to instill in us in this passage?
6. **What** comfort is hidden in verse 32 that we often forget?
7. **What** should we first be seeking? What does this mean?
8. **What** promise does our Lord add to those who seek first His kingdom?
9. **Why** does he not wish us to borrow tomorrow's troubles?

When studying a book of the Bible there is a need for background information such as what's going on historically and/or politically when the book was written. Who wrote it and what do we know about that person? What do you know about the writer of this book? What is the context surrounding the parable or event? There are a lot of things we don't know about the book that biblical scholars can share with us to help us understand it. That means we need an introduction.

Needless to say, God is a genius. The books of the Bible, though written by different people at different times, connect to each other in ways we can't begin to imagine. No matter how many times we read or study them we learn new and amazing things!

The Parable of the Prodigal Son
Below is an example of a Bible Inquiry lesson for the Prodigal Son.

. Introduction
παραβολή (Greek) paraballo
What does the word mean?
What is a parable?
With what phrase do many parables start? Why do you think they start that way?
"Thy *kingdom* come. Thy will be done." For thine is the *kingdom* and the power and the glory... What does that mean? What is the kingdom of God?

Inquiry
Read The Parable of the Prodigal Son – Luke 15:1-1, 11-32
What is the setting or context of the parable?
Who is Jesus talking to and who is he talking in front of?
Describe the father.
Describe the older son.

Describe the younger son.

How are the 2 sons rebellious?

What is the older son's rebellion and what is the father's answer to that issue?

Jesus chooses his words to make a point and/or teach a lesson. Which of the sons in the parable are which of these two groups?

Digging Deeper

Read The Parable of Lost Sheep – Luke 15:1-7 and The Parable of the Lost Coin – Luke 15:8-10

What's similar about the 3 parables?

What's different about the 3 parables?

Who is the searcher or the one seeking in each of the three parables?

Where is Jesus in each parable?

Why do you think these 2 parables are before the Prodigal Son?

What are they celebrating in each parable?

Read The Parable of the Two Sons – Matthew 21:28-32

How is this similar to the prodigal son?

Thinking it Through

The father could have gone out and found his son at any time. Why doesn't he?

Why does the father allow his son to hit "rock bottom?" How does that not happen today?

Why does the father go out to the older son?

What happens if the father doesn't allow his children to hit "rock bottom?"

What happens if the father doesn't give the son his money and freedom? What would have happened if God had not allowed the serpent to tempt Eve?

What is the "help" being offered to the tax collectors and the sinners?

In The Prodigal Son, which son do you relate to the most and why?

In Mark 2:17 Jesus says, "Those who are well have no need of a physician, but those who are sick. I came not to call the righteous, but sinners." How does that verse connect with this? Who are the "healthy?"

Ultimately, what is this parable about?

There are a few things to notice in this lesson. First, the **introduction** is brief and its purpose is to put things in perspective. There is always information participants don't know looking at the text itself such as cultural or language issues. In this case an introduction to parables is a good idea unless it's been discussed in an earlier lesson.

The next section is the **inquiry** section which is where participants look closely at the text. This does not mean that we go verse by verse asking what it means or reiterating what it says. Adults don't need that the way younger children do. When we study the parables it's always helpful to know more than the story. Who is Jesus talking to and what is going on? There is a reason Jesus chose this parable for this group at this time. He is talking to one group while another listens. Who are they? How does the parable apply to both groups? Also, the father and brothers are characters that relate to those listening so we need to look closely at them.

After the basic inquiry there is a chance to **dig deeper** and see other connections so we bring in other appropriate parables and start comparing them. Parables are both simple stories and more complex stories. Children see the simple messages, but adults can understand the more complex messages such as who Jesus is in each of the parables.

Finally, we take what we've learned and we ask questions to bring the lesson into our lives in the **Thinking it Through** section. We start asking why something happens or why it does not happen. The most common consensus is that we are the younger son who is welcomed home by Jesus, but we don't always see that we are also the older son. How are we both? This is when we ask the "what if" questions to see things from a different perspective and for greater understanding. Eventually we ask the ultimate question of what the parable is about.

Doing a Bible Inquiry and not a regular Bible study takes time to prepare and to facilitate because the participants have to do the work and you have to have the discussion. Give 20 minutes to complete the questions and walk around and encourage people to work together, collecting any further questions they may have for the question jar. Don't rush them! This is not about time. When they're ready, go over the questions and make sure you give time for any insights to be shared. After questions have been gone over start the large group discussion with the Thinking it Through questions.

Social Problem

The third category of Bible Inquiry is to address a social problem such as gay marriage, transgenderism, the death penalty, abortion, living together, casual sex, etc. I've been in many adult Bible studies where most Christians know the issue is wrong and they know why, but they don't know the Bible verses that support their view. From a Bible Inquiry perspective we would address a social problem similarly to how we address a church topic: define the terms and the issue, discuss what others say about it (including other churches), and see what the Bible says, and finally determine how we should address it as Christians. The greater question for these lessons is how some churches believe what seem contrary to the Bible and use the Bible to support their views. The more that happens the more we need to know the Bible. Let's look at transgenderism.

Transgenderism	
Define the terms.	
Transgender	
Transvestite	
Transsexual	
Ideology	
Gender Identity	
Gender Expression	
Eunuch	
Define the problem.	
What is the problem with being transgender?	
How is it possible that people are or are not born that way?	
Why is being transgender a problem?	
How is transgenderism affecting society?	
How is transgenderism affecting Christians?	
What could be the result of the problem if not addressed?	
Discuss what others are saying about it.	
What does the world say about it?	
What do doctors say about it?	
What do other churches say about it?	
Discuss what scripture says about it.	
Genesis 1:27-29	
Genesis 2:23-24	
Matthew 19:6-9	
Ephesians 5:28-32	
Mark 10:6-9	
Matthew 19:12	
1 Corinthians 6:9-11	
Ultimately, what does scripture say about transgenderism?	
What was God's plan for humans and what happened to that plan?	
What is the difference between people before and after the fall?	
How might Matthew 19:12 influence how people think about transgender?	
Where does being transgender fit in the ranking of sin?	
Discuss our responsibility as Christians.	
How are we to address transgenderism?	
How are we to address those in the church with transgender feelings?	
Do we allow those going through transgender surgery into our congregation? Why or why not?	
What would Jesus do? What has Jesus already done?	

The challenge with societal problems is that they are more of a discussion of society and not so much a discussion of scripture. We can use scenarios to talk about how we might respond to someone in a particular situation or we can talk about the problem head-on. Sometimes social problems aren't much of a Bible Inquiry or study. This doesn't mean they shouldn't be discussed with adults, however, as taking the time to talk about them can remind people that God is in control and alleviate a lot of fear. We don't have all the answers, but we know that we ALL sin and fall short of the glory of God, that God loves EVERYONE, and that Jesus died for EVERYONE. When in doubt, err on the side of the gospel.

Adult Discussion Tips

For adults, Bible study leaders usually lecture because discussion, while one of the most effective means of changing how someone thinks about something or deepening their understanding of it, is an art and takes time and practice to learn (Langhoff, 2014). Discussion is an opportunity to hit an emotional nerve and make a change or a lasting impression. The goal of an adult Bible Inquiry facilitator is the same as that for adolescents: to engage participants in discussion through compelling questions and active participation, but adults don't necessarily want to catch a bean bag to speak.

A few things to keep in mind when facilitating adult discussion:

- There will nearly always be somebody who knows more than you do (even if you're the pastor) about something. Don't sweat it. Let them share what they know. It will add to the discussion.
- Consider yourself as participating in a dialogue with your peers as opposed to a professor giving a lecture.
- Don't answer your own question before they've had a chance to think about it.
- If you are the pastor, people may wait for your thoughts or opinion before sharing their own. You want them to share first; you can share your opinion at the end.
- Speak less and listen more. If you're talking all the time they're not engaged. If they're constantly taking notes they're not engaged.
- If they don't respond or seem confused, ask again in a different way.
- If they don't give a complete answer, prompt for more information or ask if anybody has anything else to add.
- Provide handouts that stimulate discussion.
- Learn to ask good questions.

As implied earlier, it's the great discussion about a topic that keeps adults engaged. They like to solve problems and think about things from different perspectives. They like to be challenged, but they haven't been for so long that there will be fear around it... for a while.

Adults have had all kinds of life experiences with people who believe many different things, especially about faith issues, and not everyone who attends a Lutheran church was raised in the Lutheran church. Even with membership classes, many people don't know what the church they attend believes or teaches. That is why it is important to challenge adults in Bible study. Nobody can talk about what they believe if they don't know what they believe.

Discussion leads to deeper understanding. It requires people to engage and participate. Don't fall into the trap of thinking that you need to bring profound teaching TO the people instead of guiding them to unravel it themselves. Adults like to use their minds. Let them struggle with what God is telling them. Challenge them. Challenge yourself!

It is much easier to discuss in a smaller group. You can have a discussion with 20-30 people without breaking into smaller groups if people are comfortable enough to speak up. Once you get 30 or more, it's time to break into smaller groups. The key to successful small groups is making sure people know what questions they need to discuss and that they have an opportunity to share with the larger class. We want to know what other people are thinking and why.

CHAPTER 18

What's a Good Question?

One of the most difficult things to teach is how to ask good questions because asking good questions is an art that needs to be practiced. Whether you're teaching teens or adults, it's important to ask questions that make students think and that challenge them.

With little kids in the narrative stage, we primarily ask questions about the story or illustrations and encourage them to tell the story back to us as accurately as possible. Then, in the knowledge stage, we ask questions that go a little deeper in describing what's going on in the story to help kids find meaning in each story. They are building their vocabularies and are able to read to learn. In the understanding stage we start asking questions that encourage them to think or reflect on the information or story and begin Bible Inquiry. In the reason and wisdom stages we are fully into Bible Inquiry and questions are essential.

Typically, in any class if a question is asked and answered and then another question is asked and answered, by the same or a different person, it is considered discussion. Discussion is not back and forth between a teacher and a student in a question/answer form. Discussion is when questions are posed and multiple people respond to each other, agreeing, disagreeing, and posing more questions.

In previous chapters we were introduced to discussion and its importance in the learning process. Now we will learn how to craft questions that start and enhance discussion.

Not All Questions are Good Questions

Good questions lead to engaging discussions and more effective assessments about what people know or understand. It has been said that there are no bad questions, but there are bad questions. Bad questions have closed answers and end discussion. Those are questions that have obvious answers, have yes/no answers, or make participants guess the answer. Guessing a word you're thinking or filling in a blank in a sentence may get a response from a participant, but are not learning opportunities.

Many Bible studies have poor questions. Sometimes it's because the author loses sight of the objective, sometimes it's because they don't recognize bad questions, and sometimes it's because there are more statements for the leaders than questions for the participants.

The questions asked can change how a person thinks about the information. Questions asked should:

- Elicit information (used with children and *least often* with adults)
- Shape understanding (used with teens and *more often* with adults)
- Press for reflection (used *most often* with older teens and adults)

Eliciting information includes questions such as who, what, when, where, how many, or which one? For example, who were the 12 disciples? What did Jesus do to heal the blind man? The answers to these questions can be found directly in the text and are too obvious for older teens and adults. That doesn't mean they don't end up in adult Bible studies, however, like this question:

According to Acts 2:39, for whom is this promise in baptism given?

(Acts 2:39 - For the promise is for you and for your children and for all who are far off, everyone whom the Lord our God calls to himself.") Obviously, the verse itself is the answer. This is NOT *a challenging question!*

The *only* time to ask questions to elicit information with teens and adults is to remind the class of something learned previously or to have them recall something they learned in confirmation. We don't want to waste time asking questions to which everyone already knows the answer because it's right in front of them.

Questions that *shape understanding* may be used more often with teens and adults. These questions ask what they believe and involve inferences, Biblical support, and motives or causes. Examples of questions that shape understanding are:

- Why don't some Christian parents baptize their children?
- What are the benefits of baptism?
- What role does repentance play in baptism?

Questions that *press for reflection* should be used most often with older teens and adults. These questions ask why they believe what they believe and may require some thought and further study. Examples of questions that press for reflection are:

- Why do Lutherans consider baptism a sacrament and other churches do not?
- Why is it important for you that your grandchildren are baptized?
- What would happen if your unbaptized grandchild died?

Good questions should be well thought-out in advance and crafted to reach specific objectives. Bloom's Revised Taxonomy of Verbs is a great tool to use when thinking of questions and making sure they encourage thought. The following are an adaptation of the question objectives developed from Bloom's Revised Taxonomy by Morgan and Saxton (1994) to religious education.

REMEMBERING—Objective: to remember or recall facts or details. Questions that tell what the student already knows or remembers typically begin with who, what, when, or where. These questions are important because without this information, the student has nothing about which to think, talk or reflect (Langhoff, 2014).

- Who did Jesus raise from the dead?
- Who was David's first son?
- Which king came after David?
- What item went with Joshua and his army to the battle of Jericho?
- Where did Paul go on his first journey?
- Define sin.
- What is an epistle?
- Identify the twelve tribes of Israel.

UNDERSTANDING—Objective: to help find out what students understand. Questions that show what students understand need to be more complicated as they push the student to think about the facts with more depth. They shape understanding (Langhoff, 2014).

- In your own words, tell me what justification means.
- What is the difference between killing and murdering?
- Explain why Jesus needed to be perfect to pay for our sins.
- What do we NOT know about the story?
- What is the purpose of prayer?
- How do you think his life changed?

APPLYING—Objective: to apply information to different situations.
Questions that show that information can be applied to multiple situations
need to be worded in a way that helps students bring the information into
their own lives. These questions press for reflection (Langhoff, 2014).

- What would happen if nobody followed the Ten Commandments?
- What examples in your life can you find that show how Christians disrespect Jesus?
- What would you do or say if Jesus asked you why you should be allowed into heaven?
- Why do you think God kept Adam and Eve from re-entering the Garden of Eden?
- How do you know God answers *your* prayers?

**ANALYZING—Objective: to support opinion with reasoning and
ideas.** If the goal is to have a deep understanding of the information,
students need to be able to draw conclusions about situations and be able
to support them with logical reasons. These questions expect students to
show deeper understanding (Langhoff, 2014).

- Why do you think God let Eve take a bite of the fruit?
- God is good and everything good comes from God. Give three specific examples of what the world might be like without the existence of God.
- Who do you admire most in this story and what makes you admire that person?
- What if Noah let some of the people into the ark when it started to rain?
- If God sent His Son to die for everyone, can we assume that everyone will be in heaven? Why or why not?
- What are some reasons people might give for not believing Jesus was the Messiah while He was on earth?

**EVALUATING—Objective: to consider the information and be able
to make a judgment about it.** Students need to be able to summarize
information in order to defend an opinion, criticize the opinion of others,
or make a valid argument. The answers to these questions may not
necessarily be right or wrong, but it is important for them to have an
opinion and be able to support that opinion (Langhoff, 2014).

- How is the faith of the people of the Old Testament different or the same as those in the New Testament and those of us today?
- If one of the Ten Commandments is more important than the others, which would it be and why?

- What is your opinion of the Pharisees?
- What qualities make you want to admire Peter or Paul more?
- Why was Peter right or wrong to defend Jesus? What do you think you would have done in his situation?
- Why does it matter or not matter if your friends know Jesus?
- If it were possible, what would the perfect Christian's life look like?

CREATING—Objective: to take separate elements and create a whole. This objective is to help students take the separate pieces of information and put them together to create a whole thought (Langhoff, 2014).

- In your opinion, what are the three most important things every Christian needs to know?
- What would you say to a friend who asked what you believe?
- Choose five words to describe God… Jesus… the Holy Spirit.
- Describe the apostle Paul by the characteristics of his personality. What kind of guy was he?

Typical Bible Study

You don't need to write all your own Bible studies, but it's important to be able to recognize good and bad questions and to be able to add better questions. The outline of a typical published Bible study on forgiveness (Broge, 2013) is shown on the left side of the table below, the analysis of the questions is on the right.

As We Forgive…	Matthew 6:5-15
Opening – The Lord's Prayer What is forgiveness?	This is a good intro question. There will be various answers.
What does it mean when we pray "forgive us our trespasses as we forgive those who trespass against us?"	This is a good question as well, however, in order to answer it, students need some background information.
Discussion In between these questions is a lot of text to be read or said.	Note that there are VERY few questions in this study.
1. Is forgiveness an option for Christians?	1. Yes/No question. Kills discussion.
2. In light of verses 14-15, has grace now become indebted to some work we must do – specifically forgiving others? Do we earn some part of our forgiveness by forgiving?	2. Oddly worded, but is a good question. The second part is also a good question, but it is a yes/no question.
3. Describe the forgiveness we receive from God.	3. This could be a guessing question if you expect a specific answer, which

	this one does. It is a good question if students read Bible passages first and have to search for the 5 answers.
4. Do we forgive this way? 5. Is our salvation then in danger?	4. Yes/No question. Kills discussion. 5. Yes/No question. Kills discussion
Closing End with Lord's Prayer or Psalm 51:10-12.	When you have yes/no questions the class has a tendency to become very short.

So, what are some more appropriate questions? First we have to assume that the students can read. It's not necessary to ask what every verse is saying. Below are a few questions that will lead to deeper thinking:

- Often people have a misunderstanding of what forgiveness is and isn't; what is it not?
- What if we find ourselves in a position where we can't bring ourselves to forgive?
- We seek forgiveness. Why is forgiveness so important to us?
- What does it mean if we say we are people who forgive "generously and without hesitation?"
- The Lord's Prayer says "we forgive those who trespass against us." Does that mean we are commanded to forgive whether or not we feel it? Whether or not they deserve it? What good is forgiveness if we don't want to do it?
- What do our feelings have to do with forgiveness? Can we separate the two? If so, how?
- How does one forgive if they don't want to forgive?
- Think about the magnitude of sin we constantly commit. In spite of ALL our sin, God has already forgiven it. How does that make it easier or harder for us to forgive those who sin against us and why?
- What does it mean for our salvation if we don't forgive?

Compare the questions in the study to the suggested questions. What differences do you see? Which questions do you think will enhance or deepen the discussion?

Another sample is the published Bible study on Comfort (Weedon, 2009) below. Again, the left side of the table below is the published questions and the analysis is on the right.

A Matter of the Heart: Comfort from God's Word in Hard Times	
Read Exodus 16:1-30 and answer the questions. 1. **Why** did the people grumble? **What** did they fear? 2. **How** did God provide for their need?	 1. Why… What… 2. How… and one word answer.

144

Was it in an expected or unexpected manner?

3. **What** did God warn the people not to do on ~~six~~ five days of the week?

4. **Why** did they disobey Him?

5. **What** is the connection between this account and the fourth petition of the Lord's Prayer?

6. Reflect back on your life and share how God has blessed you in unexpected ways in the past. Do they give you hope for the present and future?

3. What... oddly worded and incorrect.

4. Why...

5. What...

The first five questions are directly from the text and obvious to a teen or adult who read it.

6. As many people will list things they have or good things that have happened, a question here might be what is blessing? How does God bless us? The second part is Yes/No.

Read Matthew 6:19-34

1. **Why** does our Lord warn against focusing on earthly wealth?

2. **Why** is it impossible to serve (probably meaning, to worship) both God and Mammon (wealth)?

3. Dr. Kenneth Korby once said that "Wealth is served with the liturgy of anxiety." Based on this passage what do you think he meant?

4. **What** does our Lord seek to dispel in this passage?

5. **What** does our Lord seek to instill in us in this passage?

6. **What** comfort is hidden in verse 32 that we often forget?

7. **What** should we first be seeking? What does this mean?

8. **What** promise does our Lord add to those who seek first His kingdom?

9. **Why** does he not wish us to borrow tomorrow's troubles?

1. Why...

2. Why...

3. This is a good question.

4. What...
5. What...
6. What...
7. What...
8. What...
9. Why...

Eight of these nine questions are directly from the text and obvious to a teen or adult who read it.

Read Philippians 4:9-19

1. What special promise does Paul make in verse 9?

2. What kindness did the Philippian Christians show him?

3. What is the gift, then, that Christians who have wealth can do for those who are in need?

4. What was the secret of contentment that Paul learned from "the God of

All of these questions are directly from the text and obvious to a teen or adult who read it.

peace"? 5. How did Paul encourage the Philippians to continue in the grace of giving and of sharing? 6. How does he describe their gift and what image does that suggest? [See also Romans 12:1,2] 7. What beautiful and comforting promise is provided in verse 12 (13?)? Can you claim it for yourself today?	

Unfortunately, while asking verse by verse what it says is a great way to begin preparing for a Bible study, it is not a great study as very few of the questions require thought or activity other than looking at the passage for the answer. The study is about comfort, so some of the questions should apply to how the passages help people feel God comforts them. Below are a few questions that would lead to deeper thinking and application of the verses to life:

- What does it mean or what does it look like for a Christian to be comfortable?

- People think they have more comfort or security if they have a lot of money, why is that?

- What does being able to plan for the future have to do with comfort?

- Why is it so hard for us to trust that God will provide?

- How long were the people in the wilderness before they started complaining or grumbling? Compare what the people of Israel said to Moses and Aaron to what we might complain about today?

- Do you think they had a "right" to be concerned? Why or why not?

- The people complain and God provides. What do you think the people thought?

- Did the people pass God's test? Why do you think God wants to know if they will obey Him?

- How might obeying God bring comfort to people?

- How would you feel if you were Moses and Aaron?

- After reading this account, how would it bring people comfort?

- If rich people pull away from God because they can take care of themselves and poor people pull away from God because they think He's not taking care of them, what's the answer?

- What would it look like if somebody is worshipping wealth?

- What does the life of someone look like if they are laying up treasures in heaven?

- In what areas of society do we see people choosing earthly luxuries over treasures in heaven?
- How does what we read here about money relate to the riches God gives to His chosen kings in the Old Testament?

These are only a few questions that can be written to help apply the passages to life and get students to think more deeply about them in the context of comfort.

Questions can turn a boring Bible study into an interesting and motivating Bible Inquiry. It's time, my friends, to start asking better questions and letting participants ask questions. It's time to change how we teach in the church from pastors to volunteers.

REFERENCES

A Mighty Wonder: Beginning of Time. (2019). *Enduring Faith*. St. Louis, MO: Concordia Publishing House.

American Psychological Association. (2002). *Developing Adolescents: A Reference for Professionals*. Washington, DC: American Psychological Association.

Anderson, M. (2010). *What Every 4th Grade Teacher Needs to Know*. Northeast Foundation for Children.

Anderson, M. (2011). *What Every 3rd Grade Teacher Needs to Know*. Northeast Foundation for Children.

Anderson, M. (2011). *What Every 5th Grade Teacher Needs to Know*. Northeast Foundation for Children.

Baker's Evangelical Dictionary of Bible Theology. (1996). Retrieved 2019, from www.biblestudytools.com: https://www.biblestudytools.com/dictionaries/bakers-evangelical-dictionary/hospitality.html

Blanke, M. (2016). Teaching the Faith in the Parish. *Journal of Lutheran Mission, 3*(1), 40-46.

Bonomo, V. (2017). Brain-Based Learning Theory. *Journal of Education and Human Development, 6*(1), 27-43.

Broge, J. (2013). As We Forgive... St. Louis, MO: Concordia Publishing House.

Caine, R. N., & Caine, G. (1991). *Making connections: Teaching and the human brain*. Alexandria, VA: Association for Supervision and Curriculum Development.

Calvert, S. L., & Billingsley, R. L. (1998). Young Children's Recitation and Comprehension of Information Presented by Songs. *Journal of Applied Developmental Psychology, 19*(1), 97-108.

Center for Disease Control and Prevention. (n.d.). *www.cdc.gov*. Retrieved 2018, from CDC's Developmental Milestones: https://www.cdc.gov/ncbddd/actearly/milestones/index.html

Common Core Works. (2012). *Parent Roadmaps for English Language Arts*. Washington, DC: Council of the Great City Schools. Retrieved 2018, from https://www.cgcs.org/Page/330

Early Childhood-Head Start Task Force. (2002). *Teaching Our Youngest: A Guide for Preschool Teachers and CHild Care and Family Providers*. Washington, DC: U.S. Department of Education, U.S. Department of Health and Human Services.

Elmore, T. (2015). *Artificial Maturity: Helping kids meet the challenge of becoming authentic adults*. San Francisco, CA: Jossey-Bass.

Elwell, W. A. (Ed.). (1996). *Evangelical Dictionary of Biblical Theology*. Grand Rapids, MI: Baker Books.

Faulk, R. D. (2015). *Story Elements for Kindergarten*. Retrieved 2018, from Understanding by Design: Complete Collection: http://digitalcommons.trinity.edu/educ_understandings

Freeman, R. J. (1972). *Manners and Customs of the Bible*. Plainfield, NJ: Logos International.

Froschl, M., & Spring, B. (2005). *Raising and educating healthy boys: A report on the growing crisis in boys' education*. Educational Equity Center. Retrieved from www.edequity.org

Gnjatović, D. (2015). Stories in Different Domains of Child Development. *Research in Pedagogy, 5*(1), 84-97.

Gupta, A. (2009). Vygotskian perspectives on using dramatic play to enhance children's development and balance creativity with structure in the early childhood classroom. *Early Child Development and Care, 179*(8), 1041-1054.

Gurian, M., & Ballew, A. (2003). *The boys and girls learn differently action guide for teachers*. San Francisco, CA: Jossey-Bass.

Halpern, D. F. (2004). A Cognitive-Process Taxonomy for Sex Differences in Cognitive Abilities. *American Psychological Society, 13*(4), 135-139.

Hayes, J., Chemelski, B., & Palmer, M. (1982). Nursery rhymes and prose passages: Preschoolers' liking and short-term retention of story events. *Developmental Psychology, 18*(1), 49-56.

Hendricks, W. L. (1980). *A Theology for Children*. Broadman Press.

Herring, S., & Kapidzic, S. (2015). Teens, Gender, and Self-Presentation in Social Media. In J. D. Wright (Ed.), *International encyclopedia of social and behavioral sciences* (2 ed.). Oxford: Elsevier.

Huitt, W. (1997). *Cognitive development: Applications*. Retrieved 6 2018, from http://www.edpsycinteractive.org/topics/cogsys/piagtuse.html

Jensen, A. R. (1998). *The G factor: The science of mental ability*. New York: Praeger.

Jensen, E. (2005). *Teaching With the Brain in Mind*. Alexandria, VA: ASCD.

Jensen, F. E., & Ellis Nutt, A. (2015). *The Teenage Brain: A neuroscientist's survival guide to raising adolescents and young adults*. Toronto, Ontario: Harper Collins.

Johnson, J., & Hayes, D. (1987). Preschool children's retention of rhyming and non-rhyming text: Paraphrase and rote recitation measures. *Applied Developmental Psychology*, 317-327.

Kamp, M. (2011). *Facilitation Skills and Methods of Adult Education*. Konrad-Adenauer-Stiftung.

Kamp, M. (2011). *Facilitation Skills and Methods of Adult Education*. Kampala, Uganda: Konrad-Adenauer-Stiftung.

Krathwohl, D. R. (2002). A revision of Bloom's taxonomy: An overview. *Theory into Practice, 42*(4), 212-218.

Langhoff, L. (2014). *The Art of Teaching Confirmation*. Kindle Direct.

LCMS Online Cyclopedia. (n.d.). Retrieved from www.lcms.org: http://cyclopedia.lcms.org/

Lieb, S. (1991). *Principles of adult learning*. Phoenix: Vision-South Mountain Community College.

Lohmeyer, J. W. (2015). *Now is the Time for Parish Education*. St. Louis, MO: The LCMS Reporter.

Mayo Clinic. (n.d.). *Body dysmorphic disorder: Diagnosis and treatment*. Retrieved April 4, 2019, from Mayo Clinic: https://www.mayoclinic.org/diseases-conditions/body-dysmorphic-disorder/diagnosis-treatment/drc-20353944?p=1

Mayo Clinic. (n.d.). *Body dysmorphic disorder: Symptoms and causes*. Retrieved April 4, 2019, from Mayo Clinic: https://www.mayoclinic.org/diseases-conditions/body-dysmorphic-disorder/symptoms-causes/syc-20353938?p=1

McNeely, C., & Blanchard, J. (2009). *The Teen Years Explained*. Baltimore, MD: Center for Adolescent Health.

Medina, J. (2008). *Brain rules: 12 principles for surviving and thriving at work, home, and school*. Seattle, WA: Pear Press.

Miranda, D. (2013). The role of music in adolescent development. *International Journal of Adolescence and Youth, 18*(1), 5-22.

National Research Counsil. (1999). *How People Learn: Brain, Mind, Experience, and School*. Washington, DC: The National Academies Press.

No Child Left Behind. (2005). *Helping your child through early adolescence*. Washington, DC: U.S. Department of Education.

Orey, M. (2010). *Emerging Perspectives on Learning, Teaching, and Technology*. Zurich, Switzerland: Jacobs Foundation.

Ostroff, W. L. (2012). *Understanding How Young Children Learn*. Alexandria, VA: ASCD.

Ramsey, R. (2011). *Behold the Lamb of God*. Nashville, TN: Rabbit Room Press.

Regnerus, M., Smith, C., & Smith, B. (2004). Social Context in the development of adolescent religiosity. *Applied Developmental Science, 8*(1), 27-38.

Rosen, L. D., Lim, A., Felt, J., Carrier, L., Cheever, N., Lara-Ruiz, J., . . . Rokkum, J. (2014). Media and technology use predicts ill-being among children, preteens and teenagers independent of the negative health impacts of exercise and eating habits. *Computers in Human Behavior, 35*, 364-375.

Sax, L. (2006). Six degrees of separation: What teachers need to know about the emerging science of sex differences. *Educational Horizons, 84*(3), 190-200.

Schilf, C. (2012). Rebekah Serves at the Well. *Growing in Christ*. St. Louis, MO: Concordia Publishing House.

Schurgin Okeefe, G., Clarke-Pearson, K., & Council on Communications and Media. (2011). *The Impact of Social Media on Children, Adolescents, and Families*. American Academy of Pediatrics. Retrieved from www.pediatrics.org/cgi/doi/10.1542/peds.2011-0054

Seidman, G. (2016). *Do Facebook "Likes" Affect Psychological Well-Being?* Retrieved April 15, 2019, from Psychology Today: https://www.psychologytoday.com/us/blog/close-encounters/201610/do-facebook-likes-affect-psychological-well-being

Shaffer, D. R., & Kipp, K. (2010). *Developmental Psychology: Childhood and Adolescence* (8th ed.). Belmont, CA: Cengage Learning.

Turan, F., & Ulutas, I. (2016). Using Story Books as Character Education Tools. *Journal of Education and Practice, 7*(15), 169-176.

Vawter, D. (2010). Mining the middle school mind. *Education Digest, 75*(5), 47-49.

Wallace, W. T. (1994). Memory for music: Effect of melody on recall of text. *Journal of Experimental Psychology: Learning, Memory and Cognition, 20*(6), 1471-1485.

Web MD. (2018). *3-4 -Year-Old Developmental Milestones: Cognitive, Language, and Motor Skills.* Retrieved 2018, from https://www.webmd.com/parenting/3-to-4-year-old-milestones?print=true

Weedon, W. C. (2009). A Matter of the Heart: Comfort from God's Word in Hard Times. St. Louis, MO: Concordia Publishing House.

Weinschenk, S. (2012). *Why We're All Addicted to Texts, Twitter and Google.* Retrieved April 15, 2019, from Psychology Today: https://www.psychologytoday.com/us/blog/brain-wise/201209/why-were-all-addicted-texts-twitter-and-google

Willingham, W. W., & Cole, N. (1997). *Gender and Fair Assessment.* Hillsdale, NJ: Erlbaum.

Wilson, M. (2010). *What Every 2nd Grade Teacher Needs to Know.* Northeast Foundation for Children.

Wilson, M. (2011). *What Every 1st Grade Teacher Needs to Know.* Northeast Foundation for Children.

Wood, C. (2018). *Yardsticks: Child and Adolescent Development Ages 4-14.* Turners Falls, MA: Center for Responsive Schools.

ABOUT THE AUTHOR

Laura Langhoff Arndt is the author of *The Art of Teaching Confirmation, I Am Jesus' Little Lamb,* and is the woman behind the Carpenter's Ministry Toolbox, a Christian education resource ministry whose goal is to apply current educational research and strategies to congregational education. She dreams of equipping and encouraging pastors, other professional church workers, and volunteers to effectively educate God's children from preschool through adult. Laura is a professional educator with an M.A. in classroom instruction, administrative leadership experience, as well as Director of Christian Education (DCE) certification in the LCMS.

One of her many passions is to visit with both professional and volunteer church educators in person through workshops providing educational resources, support, and encouragement. Laura lives in Sterling, NE and enjoys painting watercolors and riding her bike.

More free resources are available at
www.carpentersministrytoolbox.com

68226304R00088

Made in the USA
Columbia, SC
07 August 2019